Children with Disabilities and their Families:

a review of research

Mark Philp
and
Derek Duckworth

NFER-Nelson

Published by The NFER-Nelson Publishing Company Ltd.,
Darville House, 2 Oxford Road East,
Windsor, Berks. SL4 1DF.

First Published 1982
Crown Copyright 1982.
Not to be reproduced in whole or in part without the permission
of the Department of Health and Social Security.
ISBN 0-7005-0491-5
Code 8133 02 1

Photoset in Times by Illustrated Arts
Printed in Great Britain by
Unwin Brothers Limited The Gresham Press Old Woking Surrey
A member of the Staples Printing Group

Distributed in the USA by Humanities Press Inc.,
Atlantic Highlands, New Jersey 07716 USA

Contents

List of Tables and Figures

Acknowledgements

We would both like to express our gratitude to the Physical Disablement Research Liaison Group of the Department of Health and Social Security for their support of this work at all stages. We also thank Mrs E. V. Browne and Mrs S. M. Woodward of the Health Services Research Unit, University of Kent for typing and retyping several drafts. In addition, Mark Philp would like to thank the Department of Applied Social Studies at Bradford for their assistance during his stay, with special thanks to Professor Hilary Rose and Dr Wallace McCulloch.

Abbreviations

A number of abbreviations are used throughout the text. These are listed below:

Ar	=	Arthritis
As	=	Asthma
CF	=	Cystic Fibrosis
CP	=	Cerebral Palsy
D	=	Diabetes
DS	=	Down's Syndrome
MD	=	Muscular Dystrophy
SB	=	Spina Bifida
Th	=	Thalidomide

Introduction

This book offers a review of the research on the social and emotional problems experienced by children with physical impairments and their families. The review takes into account the research extant in the field up to 1978. It is, in effect, a summary, condensation and revision of a report written by one of us (Mark Philp) at the end of 1978 for the Department of Health and Social Security under the title, *Physically Handicapped Children and their Families*. The Department agreed to finance a one-year research fellowship in the School of Applied Social Studies at the University of Bradford in order to ascertain how far existing research was able to answer questions in the following four fields:

1. Information systems
2. Service distribution and use
3. The role of the voluntary sector
4. The link between disablement in children and social and emotional difficulties for these children and their families.

In order to narrow the field it was agreed that, as far as possible, material relating to sensory impairments, mental retardation and educational handicaps should be excluded from the review. It was also felt that the review should concentrate on British material of reasonably recent origin.

The completed review proved somewhat lengthy, reflecting the amount of information available and its lack of comparability. Because its bulk rendered the report unsuitable for wide dissemination the Department asked a seconded researcher (Derek Duckworth) to provide a much briefer version for use within the

Department. This version necessarily had to omit much of the sociological and philosophical discussion which had been offered in the original. Consequently, when the question was raised of providing a version for a wider audience we decided to collaborate and to broaden the abridged version. By doing this we were able both to bring in some of the omitted material which we both felt it important to offer for wider discussion and to provide a perspective on the research cited by using the scheme of 'disablement' terminology recently suggested for trial use by the World Health Organization. This book is the result of our continuing dialogue about how social research can contribute to some of the central problems involved in understanding the difficulties of children with impairments, disabilities and handicaps. Consequently, it is not simply a collection of facts and figures gleaned from previous reports, but is an attempt to present an argument about how the community might develop an understanding of the problems of these children and their families and about how it should be trying to help to solve them. The main argument for our case appears in the first and the final chapters, but it should be clear that its validity rests equally on the evidence which we offer in the intervening chapters.

Finally, we would remark that, though we have been rather critical of much of the work which has been done in this field, we also wish to stress that it was through the efforts of individual and sometimes isolated researchers that the interest of those who have subsequently followed them, ourselves included, was awakened. Indeed, without them, health professionals and researchers would not be in a position today to recognize both how little they know and how much they need to know, if they are to respond to the needs of children with disabilities appropriately and efficiently. Our criticisms are made with hindsight and an eye to the future, but both hindsight and conceptions of the future are built on the materials of the past, so that, in a very real sense, our fundamental debt is to those whose work we now wish to see improved upon.

Mark Philp, Jesus College, Oxford
Derek Duckworth, Health Services Research Unit,
   University of Kent
November 1981

CHAPTER ONE
The Meaning of Disablement

Definitions of 'handicap'

The terms 'handicap' and 'handicapped' as used today in Britain
carry several meanings; some of these reflect formal attempts at
definition of many years ago. A recent report of a World Health
Organization (WHO) Working Group entitled *Early Detection of
Handicap in Children* (WHO, 1980a) mentions one such early
British attempt at definition in which 'handicaps' were regarded as a
subset of 'disabilities'; a handicap being 'a disability affecting normal growth, development and adjustment to life over a substantial
period of time, if not permanently'. Similarly, 'disabilities' were
defined as a subset of 'defects', a disability being 'a defect which
results in some malfunction but which does not necessarily affect the
individual's normal life'. A defect was defined as 'some infection,
impairment or disorder of the body, intellect or personality'.

The working group point out that these definitions were not
found to be very useful because they relied on 'subjective considerations'. Presumably, they were felt to be insufficiently precise for
professional use by medical and health workers. However, these
definitions correspond fairly closely to those used today by most
people. That of handicap has obvious appeal: a person who has had
a defect or a chronic illness resulting in malfunction from childhood
is indeed not unlikely to have a 'handicap' and to be 'handicapped'
in the sense of the definition.

The WHO working group attempt an improved conceptualization of handicap by conceiving it in broad terms as 'some sort of
long-term disadvantage', and then by dividing it into 'intrinsic' and
'extrinsic' handicap. The former is described as 'disadvantage aris-

ing from the individual's own characteristics from which he cannot be separated' and the latter as 'disadvantage arising from environment and circumstances', a distinction emphasized by Agerholm (1975) in her proposals for a terminology and classification of handicaps. However, the group does not make use of this particular approach with any great conviction and seems to find another dichotomization – that between 'primary' and 'secondary' handicap – of greater practical use, partly because secondary handicap is regarded as covering an important facet of disadvantage, i.e. adverse professional and public reaction to the presence of primary handicap by way of labelling and stigma. The intrinsic/extrinsic distinction seems of less significance to the working group except that it serves to delimit roughly the main concerns of 'medical' and 'social' workers, the former dealing with intrinsic and the latter with extrinsic handicap.

An alternative terminology

The main weakness of the working group's exposition of handicap seems to be that, just as in the early definition they criticize, the concept is vastly overloaded with meaning. A better approach, perhaps, is implicit in the group's suggestion that a 'disability' only becomes a 'handicap' if the individual is unable to develop compensatory strategies. At present, children born with some mental or physical defect are labelled as 'handicapped' before they are old enough to develop such strategies. Yet in these days there are many adults, and children too, born with substantial defects, who by determination, persistence, prostheses, skilful rehabilitation, favourable circumstances etc. do not become 'handicapped'.

A possible way through this problem is provided by means of a trial scheme of terminology recently published by the WHO (1980b) following preparatory work undertaken in Britain by Wood (1975). This scheme provides the conceptual base for a trial 'International Classification of Impairments, Disabilities, and Handicaps' (ICIDH) but its merits can be considered separately from the Classification. In the scheme, the idea of handicap as equivalent to disadvantage consequent on disease, defect or disability is given a much more precise definition by means of a terminology of 'disablement' (Wood and Badley, 1978). Disablement is regarded as consisting of three consecutive but distinguishable 'planes' of experience – that of impairment, that of disability and that of handicap. The three planes are linked together as shown in Figure 1 but, if we do not wish to distinguish them, 'disablement' is the proposed collective term (Wood, 1980). This is, in fact, the formula we most commonly adopt in this study.

Figure 1: The concepts in the WHO trial scheme

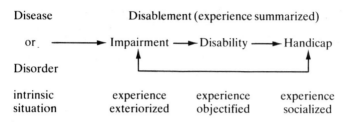

The main justification given in the ICIDH for conceiving disablement in this way is that the diseases and disorders which are amenable to prevention and cure, the classical medical activities, account for a diminishing proportion of mankind's ill-health. Medicine has been successful in eradicating or limiting a whole range of infectious diseases. By contrast, the disorders which mainly need management have come to dominate morbidity experience, at least in developed countries. As examples of this experience, the Introduction to the ICIDH (*op.cit.*, p. 9) cites 'the effects of trauma, impairments of special sense organs, mental retardation and mental illness and the chronic diseases of middle and later life, particularly heart disease, stroke, bronchitis and arthritis'. Many workers among children, since they are often concerned especially with children's educational development in school settings, will take particular note of mental retardation in this list, though 'intellectual impairment' appears to be the preferred term within the ICIDH itself. In the ICIDH, a sound foundation for conceptualizing disablement is laid by the careful definitions provided for experience within the three planes. Thus:

  i. 'impairments' are abnormalities of bodily structure and appearance and of organ or system function;

ii.   'disabilities' are restrictions on the performance of those functions and activities which are characteristic of human beings; and

iii.   'handicaps' are disadvantages preventing the fulfilment of roles that are normal (depending on age, sex and social and cultural factors) for that individual.

It follows that in this scheme 'handicaps', for instance, are not now to be thought of as a sub-set of disabilities, but as disadvantages *resulting from* disabilities. In consequence, the trial WHO 'classification' really consists of three separate classifications: one of impairments, one of disabilities, and one of handicaps.

A feature of the classification of handicaps is that the individual's experience of disablement on this plane is to be described in terms of six specified dimensions: (i) orientation, (ii) physical independence, (iii) mobility, (iv) occupation, (v) social integration and (vi) economic self-sufficiency. In this way, considerable flexibility without an over-precise dichotomization into intrinsic and extrinsic handicap is achieved. Certainly, the first three of these dimensions clearly relate mainly to the perspectives of medical and paramedical professionals, but they do not exclusively do so. Similarly, the last three relate mainly, but not exclusively, to social and psychological perspectives. As a result of this balance, there is less danger of the latter perspectives being ignored, a common failing of purely 'medical' terminological schemes.

Advantages of the WHO scheme

Clear terminology is always an aid to effective communication, especially between groups of people, such as medical and behavioural scientists, who have different perspectives on the matter at issue. Even though it may be still rather medically orientated, the WHO scheme provides an advance on the present terminology. It is, therefore, an aid to clear thinking about the role of medical workers *vis a vis* social workers and vice versa.

Other related practical advantages are not difficult to find. Thus it has been a weakness of many individual pieces of research into children's disablement (impairment/disability/handicap) that their scope has been unduly circumscribed by the traditional medical viewpoint at the outset. Sometimes indeed, research into 'handicap' in children has hardly touched on disablement at all but has concentrated on diseases, disorders and defects, and upon the 'popular' ones among these. That different diseases, etc. often lead to disabilities and handicaps common to all of them has often gone virtually unremarked. In consequence, the possibilities for common, and therefore more economic, provision for remedying or alleviating these disabilities and handicaps have sometimes not been recognized.

Again, the terminology enables us to verbalize and therefore analyse commonplace experience. Impairments are the outward and visible signs of a pathological state; disabilities are what the child cannot do (or does to excess) in consequence of his or her impairments, while handicaps are the disadvantages and discordances in certain important dimensions of experience which stem from the presence of impairments and disabilities. Consider a newly-born child having, say, a loss of auditory sensitivity. In due course, the impairment can be detected and later still it can be measured functionally in terms of mean hearing-threshold level over specified frequencies. In the child's first year of life, certain disabilities, shown by lack of response to the mother's voice, may well be beginning to emerge. In terms of the WHO trial classification of disabilities these are 'listening' disabilities, but later speaking disabilities and various kinds of behaviour disabilities may well develop. At about the same time, or later, handicap in several dimensions could well occur. It is likely, for instance, that when they go to school many children with severe loss of auditory sensitivity will suffer some form of educational disadvantage unless special provision is made. This provision might well involve the child's family in extra costs, but in terms of the WHO scheme this will only be a handicap if the family (or the school) cannot afford these costs. In the particular case, this kind of 'economic self-sufficiency' handicap, it is to be hoped, is temporary and removable. It is not a fixed invariable 'intrinsic' property; rather, its occurrence and removal is profoundly influenced by societal norms, values and action.

In other words, under the new WHO scheme, 'handicap' is not a label that should be automatically and permanently applied to any child with impairments, however severe. Rather it should be used as a precise description of last-resort disadvantage and unmet needs. Parents whose children have impairments should no longer be advised to send their children to a special school because they are 'handicapped', but because at a special school they will be given help and teaching of a kind which will remove or at least alleviate one or more of their 'handicaps'.

In summary, as is pointed out in the manual describing the WHO classification (WHO, 1980b), three important features of the 'new' concept of handicap should be borne in mind:

i.   Some value is attached to departure from a structural, functional or performance norm, either by the individual himself or by his peers in a group to which he relates;

ii. The valuation is dependent on cultural norms, so that a person may be handicapped in one group and not in another – time, place, status and role are all contributory;

iii. In the first instance, the valuation is usually to the disadvantage of the affected individual. (*op.cit.*, p. 29).

The quotation is worth continuing because the richness of the concept of handicap when conceived of in this way is explained further.

The state of being handicapped is relative to other people – hence the importance of existing societal values, which, in turn, are influenced by the institutional arrangements of society. Thus, the attitudes and responses of the non-handicapped plays a central part in modelling the ego-concept, and defining the possibilities, of an individual who is potentially handicapped – the latter has a very limited freedom to determine or modify his own reality . . .

Handicap is characterized by a discordance between the individual's performance or status and the expectations of the particular groups of which he is a member. Disadvantage accrues as a result of his being unable to conform to the norms of his universe. Handicap is thus a social phenomenon, representing the social and environmental consequences for the individual stemming from the presence of impairments and disabilities. The essence of an adverse valuation by society is discrimination by other people, but the concept is, nevertheless, essentially neutral as regards its origins. Thus the individual's own intention is of no immediate concern; disadvantage can arise when the individual deviates in spite of his own wishes, but it can also develop when the deviation is inadvertent or as the product of his own choice (*ibid.*).

The parental experience of handicap

It may be seen in some quarters as a defect of the WHO scheme that it is still too 'medical'. Sociologists may feel that the concept of handicap as developed within it is ostensibly concerned only with direct health-related experience and those aspects of disadvantage which can be identified as stemming more or less directly from identified impairments and disabilities in the individual person. Thus, obviously important aspects of social deprivation such as poverty and poor housing are not among the six dimensions of handicap provided by the classification. Rather these are seen as factors which might exacerbate handicap by interacting with impairments and disabilities. The stated justification for this approach is that otherwise 'dilution of the concept of handicap . . . tends to confound identification of specific health-related experiences and the means by which these might be controlled' (*op.cit.*, p. 34). It is plain, then, that the implied model of disease and its consequences is still primarily 'medical' rather than 'social', though it can be argued that this approach is wholly justified in the context for which the WHO classification was designed.

Similarly, the locus of specific handicaps is the individual who experiences disease, impairment and disability rather than those others who, because of their relationships with that individual, find themselves, in turn, at a disadvantage of some kind. Hence, in terms of the WHO classifications and in the context of the subject of this book, it is only the child who is handicapped or, better, 'has handicaps', not his parents, siblings, relatives and friends. Nevertheless, just as an alternative 'social' analysis of people's experience might legitimately in some contexts treat poverty, etc. as a handicap, so the parents etc. of a child with handicaps might themselves be regarded as having handicaps.

Sociological analyses from this perspective are not uncommon and while in some ways they do not fit in particularly well with the conceptual framework of the WHO scheme, they can use its language. The kind of perspective offered by, say, Berger and Luckman (1967), or Booth (1978) implies that children who are born with a defect or impairment do not themselves necessarily experience the full force of the consequent handicaps because, having no previous experience, they have no expectations to be threatened. By contrast, their parents are suddenly and inescapably faced with a situation which violates their taken-for-granted assumptions about the natural order of things.

To develop this theme further at this point is inappropriate, but our reading of the literature is such that the experience of the families, especially the parents, of the child who is born with or has acquired impairments, seems to require particular emphasis. We shall therefore return to both parental and sibling experience of 'handicap' in later chapters of this review. Indeed, in Chapters Three and Four and again in the final chapter, we shall discuss the parental experience in some depth. At this point we shall revert to a discussion of another aspect of a problem we have already touched upon – that of the effects on research strategy generally of being bound by the limited medical model focussing on disease and its manifestations.

The scope of research on children with disablement

As the preceding discussion implies one far-reaching effect of the dominance of the traditional medical model has been to leave the area of disablement experience bereft of an adequate conceptual framework. This has had particularly severe effects on research in the area because it has led researchers, or, more probably, their funding bodies, to focus on disablement as experienced only within a range of interest defined by particular medically-identifiable conditions. The main impression given by the research, at least as it concerns children with disablement, is, therefore, that much research has been concentrated on children with this or that disease or disorder and that it is often supported by funding bodies or pressure groups who feel a responsibility towards 'their' particular group of children.

Undoubtedly, it is natural and inevitable that this should happen, but it does mean that, overall, there has been little by way of coherent planning, and very limited liaison either between researchers who work for different institutions or between the institutions themselves. In consequence, the research as a whole does not fit together in terms of aims pursued, problems to be solved or questions to be answered. Hence another unfortunate consequence of what amounts to a fragmentary approach is that researchers and their sponsors sometimes give the impression of not being particularly interested in contributing to the development of an overall perspective of what it means to be a child with disablement or to care for such a child, unless that child belongs to 'their' group.

This approach could be changed by drawing samples defined by ICIDH categories so that researchers can develop hypotheses and gather data in such a way that more general conclusions will emerge. If we still wish to show how the disablement experiences of children with a particular medically-identified condition vary, then we can persist in identifying the population in terms of medical symptomatology. But if we are trying to determine when disease generally begins to have an impact on the child's functioning, or on that of his family, then we shall identify the population at the level of disability or, more radically, at the level of specific dimensions of handicap.

Of course, even with the ICIDH to help us, there will still be problems, but it is a hopeful sign that in recent years even without the benefit of the ICIDH, certain quite large scale researches with this broad focus have been undertaken, such as those relating to the Family Fund and those conducted at Bristol. Further, the problems which will arise with the new perspective are identifiable and the decisions that have to be made are within the competence of researchers and research managers. Thus they will have to make decisions, still rather arbitrary, about what aspects, kinds or degrees of disablement are to count towards membership of that population. Or again, they will have to decide where to draw the line, for instance, between illness on the one hand and disability, with its aura of permanence, on the other. They will also have to decide whether to focus on impairment, disability, handicap, or all three. The kinds of question that might arise are 'at what point does a particular impairment, disability or handicap become serious enough to count as disablement?' or 'Does one include children with a mild intellectual impairment (an IQ of just below 70) in a study of children with mental retardation just because the International Classification of Impairments, Disabilities and Handicaps (ICIDH) defines such an impairment in this way (WHO, 1980, p. 53)?' In fact, researchers will have to decide how much of the

ICIDH, with its carefully drawn distinctions between impairment, disability and handicap, they can take on board. Certainly, if they do decide to make use of it, they will find that the link between the medically-defined condition and the ultimate handicap, hitherto virtually axiomatic, can become very tenuous indeed. Many children with diseases, though inevitably impaired, are not disabled or handicapped, and many are seriously disabled and handicapped who are only minimally impaired. Further, as is suggested earlier in the chapter, the link between disability and handicap is not always very strong because handicap is often much more closely related to the social and environmental circumstances surrounding the person than to the impairments and disabilities of the person notionally 'handicapped'.

There are, of course, no answers which are 'right' for every researcher on every piece of research to the questions stated or implied in the preceding paragraph. Better and worse answers are distinguished by the extent to which they help us to achieve certain goals. But if our goal is to reduce the disabilities and alleviate the handicaps of all children with disablement, then the model of disablement experience suggested by the ICIDH is a marked advance on the traditional approach of labelling all severely impaired children as 'handicapped'. It is an advance in that it encourages researchers to abandon disease-based samples and to look instead for samples which allow generalizations to broader populations of children with disablement and their families. Seeing a move in this direction as desirable is not to disregard the fact that the decision regarding sampling are, at least in part, a function of the researchers' assumptions, intuitions, knowledge and experiences and of the 'state of the art' at the time.

CHAPTER TWO
The Practical Problems of Caring for a Child with Disablement

Introduction

The material in this chapter is derived more from the straight-forward fact-finding kind of research sponsored by organizations of various kinds for their own purposes rather than from the theoreti-cally-based, hypothesis-testing kind of research which is more characteristic of research carried out in research institutes and by research units within institutions of higher education. In consequence, though the research reported in this chapter has often been most carefully carried out so that the data are reliable, some lack of generalizability across time, place and disorder is evident. How-ever, readers will notice that, where we can, we make considerable use of the work of Butler *et al.* (1976, 1978) and of Bradshaw and his colleagues (see, Bradshaw, Baldwin, Glendinning and 'Family Fund' in the references). This is mainly because these researchers carry out research which, whilst it is empirical and focuses on selec-ted topics, does look at broad samples of children with disablement and their families, which is, after all, the focus of this review.

The adequacy of housing

There is evidence that the housing of families with a child with dis-ablement is often inadequate (Fox, 1971; Walker *et al.*, SB: 1971; Richards and McIntosh, SB: 1973). Kew (1973) has suggested that many families ought to change their accommodation to cater for the child. However, evidence that families with such a child occupy worse housing than comparable groups in the general population is not so clear, though Spain (1973), Laurence (1976) and Anderson and Spain (1977) have undertaken work in this area relating to children with spina bifida. Spain (*op.cit.*) reports that she found a higher proportion of her sample living in council and private rented accommodation than that found in a comparable Greater London Council survey. Hence, the evidence available on the inadequacy of housing may reasonably be summarized as follows: families with children with disablement are more likely than families without such children to experience poor housing conditions where the incidence of disablement has a social class bias (e.g. that arising from spina bifida) and where disposable income is reduced through the costs of caring for the child.

On a related issue – the actual proportion of these families living in housing which is unsuitable because of the nature of the child's disablement – evidence is available, but there is considerable variation between the results provided by different studies. The main reasons for the variation seem to be simply that children with different forms of disablement have different housing needs and that the relevant studies are, on the whole, confined to the child population with particular diseases and disorders. For example, Cull (1974) and Burton (1975), whose surveys of children with cystic fibrosis will be referred to several times in this review, suggest that there are no special housing needs associated with disablement in children with this condition. On the other hand, Woodburn (1973), studying children with spina bifida, estimated from her sample that as high a proportion as 72 per cent were living in unsuitable housing, though she does observe that much of this figure reflects defects in the housing generally available. From broader samples, Butler *et al.* (1978) estimated that between six and fifteen per cent of families were living in unsuitable housing, whereas Glendinning and Bradshaw (1977) give a figure of 37 per cent. To some extent, the evidence on families moving because of the needs of the child supports the higher range of figures: both Hunt (SB: 1973) and Baldwin (1977) report that a third of their samples moved for this reason. Woodburn (SB: 1973) gives a figure of 47 per cent with 26 per cent seeking a second move because their new housing failed to meet their needs.

The type of housing occupied is obviously linked with families' satisfaction and dissatisfaction though, as categorization in most studies is simply in terms of local authority versus private ownership, clear-cut relevant findings can hardly be expected to emerge.

The Family Fund's research (Glendinning and Bradshaw, 1977) showed that about 50 per cent of families with a child with disablement live in council accommodation, while the General Household Survey's data show that only a third of families as a whole live in such accommodation. The Family Fund research also showed that families with a child with disablement in council housing were more likely to be rehoused than were families as a whole. Even so, they were just as likely to regard their housing as unsuitable.

As has been pointed out above, variations between studies arise partly because of the nature of the particular sample studied. They also stem partly from the difficulty of labelling particular accommodation as unsuitable. Do we mean that the house cannot be adapted or merely that the house has not been adapted? Butler *et al.* (1978) have attempted to be specific on this point. They found that 41 per cent of their broad sample of families with a child with disablement were adequately housed and needed no adaptations and that 44 per cent were adequately housed but needed adaptations. This leaves only 15 per cent of families to be accounted for, and Butler *et al.*'s findings suggest that three-fifths of these needed adaptations which might not be feasible, so that there was a possible need for rehousing, and that the remaining two-fifths (six per cent of the original sample) definitely needed rehousing. They also suggested that parental dissatisfaction was not an adequate indicator of the need for rehousing. Of the 33 per cent of their sample of families who wanted to move, only just over a quarter were living in housing which was definitely unsuitable or in need of adaptations which might not have been feasible. Further, half of these families in unsuitable housing lacked only an adequate number of bedrooms.

Other studies give higher estimates of the need for rehousing because figures are based only on parental dissatisfaction. Butler *et al.*'s figures have the advantage of using both an objective criterion based on wheelchair and mobility housing standards and a categorization of housing by type which gives a realistic view of the problem.

The effect of lack of mobility

Butler *et al.* (*ibid.*) identify the main housing problem in terms of lack of mobility of the child. This is obviously crucial when steps and stairs have to be negotiated, and Hewett (1970) has reported that the majority of complaints about housing related to this problem. Again Butler *et al.* report precise figures, this time in their earlier study (1976). They suggest that steps and stairs were a problem for as many as two-thirds of their sample; about a half of their sample were unable to gain access to some rooms in the house and about a third found difficulty in reaching the garden. Only about ten per cent had their bedrooms downstairs. In Butler *et al.*'s 1978 sample a more detailed breakdown of mobility problems was attempted. It was found that 40 per cent found stairs to be a major problem, 15 per cent had problems with passageways and doors, while 44 per cent had problems with bathrooms and WCs. In addition, 43 per cent had to be carried upstairs and a further 15 per cent helped upstairs.

These findings of Butler *et al.* based on survey research could be usefully supplemented by further intensive qualitative study of the matter. Jarvis (1977) has undertaken research of this kind. Though his sample was small (22), his method of evaluating mobility problems by observing and by discussing with parents the strategies they use to cope with them has much to commend it.

Aids, adaptations and equipment

When impairment leads to disability, aids to mobility and aids to other aspects of living are both required by most children who experience disablement. A few researchers have inquired into the availability of aids, into parents' perceptions of their child's experience with aids and into the value of the aids being used.

Hewett (1970) reports that, at the time of her research, almost half her sample of parents of children with cerebral palsy had no aids for the child, either because they were awaiting their arrival or because they were confused about how to obtain them. About half of the 96 with aids were experiencing difficulties with them. These difficulties usually related to the design of the aids, to their weight (especially chairs) or to the difficulties they made for the mother when, for example, she went shopping. An important point made by Hewett was that parents received aids from a variety of sources so that they often had to select aids without knowing anything about either the choice available or the criteria they should use when choosing.

Woodburn (SB: 1973) describes problems relating to the supply, management and storage of aids in some detail and gives a useful breakdown by percentage of those children with spina bifida who were having difficulty with different kinds of aid. These percentages are shown in Table 1.

Table 1: Percentage of problems with aids
(Woodburn, 1973)

Aid	%
Crutches or sticks	46
Standing tables	42
Rollators	36
Parallel bars	28
Chariots/trolleys	23
Yorkhill chairs	0

Woodburn summarizes her findings as follows:

> Special aids and equipment were, on the whole, found to be very helpful and there were very few cases where equipment was discarded as little used. There were, however, difficulties in obtaining some items needed and in their management and, for a few people with limited accommodation, there were problems with storage (*op.cit.*, p. 99).

In the more broady-based Family Fund sample (1975) only four per cent had a mobility problem for which they were not receiving an aid. However, about 35 per cent of parents felt that their child would benefit from additional aids of this kind. Aids to independence were in demand; 21 per cent of families reported that a need for these aids existed which was not being met. Also, in families where the child already used aids, 74 per cent felt that other aids were required.

Most mobility aids were provided by hospitals (21 per cent), appliance centres (12 per cent) or social services (ten per cent). Thirty-five per cent of parents reported that they received no help from any organization in obtaining aids to independence. Of those who received help of this kind, 38 per cent received it from the social services.

In general, it seems that parents lack knowledge of the sources of assistance and the range of aids available. When they have the knowledge, they still have difficulty in obtaining aids without undue delay.

Jarvis's (1977, 1978) study, of the wheelchair requirements of children with mobility problems, mentioned above, is well-argued and a control is used. He suggests that these children are frequently more handicapped than they need be. Their problems, it seems, stem partly from the environment, but they also stem from children's not being able to make the most effective use of their wheelchairs because of design faults: 'There seems to be good reason to suspect that major improvements in the outcome for the children could result from relatively minor improvements in wheelchair design, and . . . there are equally good reasons to suppose that such improvements . . . are feasible' (1978, p. 240). Jarvis's study seems to represent a commendable attempt to observe the phenomenological world of the child – to take into account the quality of the child's experience and to try to locate the barriers that can be overcome or moved to allow the children greater activity and social contact. This approach seems essential not only in the designing of aids and the adaptation of environments, but also in the allocation of aids, especially in view of Glendinning and Bradshaw's (1977) observations. These researchers have estimated that about 70 per cent of their sample of families with a child with disablement needed adaptations, though only 20 per cent had actually applied for local authority help and half of those applying had been refused. Butler *et al.* (1976) report that 38 per cent of families in their sample had had adaptations, the most common being ramps and rails.

In their later paper, Butler *et al.* (1978) found that 48 per cent of families now had adaptations. They also estimated that 46 per cent of ambulant children with disablement and just over 50 per cent of the semi-ambulant and wheelchair bound needed them. The adaptations required by the ambulant were mostly minor, but those required by other groups were quite likely to be major undertakings such as an extra bedroom/bathroom/wc on the ground floor or a stair-lift.

General problems of transport

Probably most kinds of disablement will reduce the mobility of children to some extent, though the most serious problems will obviously be faced if attempts are made to use public transport when the child suffers from gross physical incapacity or behaviour disturbance (Rutter *et al.*, 1970a; Crank and Kelly, 1976; Baldwin, 1977). Jarvis (1977) describes the alternative of walking, with the child in a wheelchair, as equally problematic, Baldwin (1975b), discusses how the kinds of disablement that follow certain disorders, such as hæmophilia and eczema, can prevent the use of public transport. The overall problem has been best explained in quantitative terms by Butler *et al.* (1978). They found that 45 per cent of mothers whose child had disablement of one kind or another never travelled with their child on public transport while a further 33 per cent had considerable difficulty when they did so.

Ownership of a car does not eliminate all problems (Harrison, 1977, p. 58), though Butler *et al.* (*op.cit.*) report that half of those without a car felt that one was essential if their child was to be mobile. Baldwin (1975b) attempted to assess the point at which the need for transport becomes significantly greater for the child with disablement than for the 'normal' child. She concluded tentatively that this occurred round about the age of two and a half years, i.e. the age at which normal children begin to contribute significantly to their own mobility.

School transport

The evidence of Butler *et al.* (1978) was, that at the time of their survey, the large majority (88 per cent) of parents of children with disablement were receiving appropriate help. Complaints referred especially to uncertain arrival times and the distance to pick-up points. The Family Fund's sample provides comparable findings: about 80 per cent of parents with children with disablement in day nurseries or playgroups and 70 per cent of those with such children in ordinary schools were satisfied with school transport (Baldwin, 1977).

Problems with the transport provided to bring children home from residential special schools or enabling parents to visit their children in these schools seem rather more serious (*ibid.*). Thus, in an earlier report, Baldwin (1975b) had suggested that many local authorities interpreted their responsibilities rather narrowly and usually paid for or provided transport at the beginning and end of terms and at mid-term. Yet schools expect and encourage parents to take their children home much more often than this. If they are implemented, certain of the Warnock Committee's recommendations should improve matters (Warnock, 1978; 8.40 and 9.20).

Hospitalization

Hospitalization is by no means a rare event for any child. Davie *et al.* (1972) record that 45 per cent of seven-year-olds had been in hospital at some time, while Fogelman (1976) gives a figure of 49 per cent for 16-year-olds from the same sample (The National Children's Bureau's Child Development Survey). It is generally accepted that hospitalization can be a disturbing experience (Stacey *et al.*, 1970) and that, if it is prolonged, it can result in developmental retardation through lack of stimulus (Rutter, 1972). Children between the age of six months and four years find hospitalization particularly stressful (Schaffer, 1974; Wolff, 1969). The most common symptom of stress is enuresis.

Obviously, the child with disablement is even more likely to be hospitalized than the 'normal' child, though the duration and frequency of admission varies considerably, even within groups of children with a particular disorder. For example, Burton found that five-year-old children with cystic fibrosis had been in hospital for a total time ranging from one to 192 weeks. Mothers reported some emotional distress in 61 per cent of the children and behaviour disturbance after returning home in 80 per cent. Cull (1974) also found wide variations in both number of admissions and duration of stay in five-year-old children with cystic fibrosis.

Among children with spina bifida the number and duration of hospitalization experiences also varies considerably. Generally, the duration of admissions fell with age (SB: Tew and Laurence, 1976). On the basis of their observations Tew and Laurence suggest that frequent short stays in hospital are less threatening to the children than fewer longer ones, though, in general, all children showed increased resentment towards doctors and hospitals as they grew older. Particularly high rates of admission are reported for children with spina bifida by several researchers (Freeston, 1971; Lorber, 1972; Hunt, 1973; Woodburn, 1973; Anderson and Spain, 1977).

Visiting children in hospital or the mother's staying in hospital with the child provides reassurance to all children, while adequate preparation of the child and the opportunity for parents to have full discussion of fears and worries both reduce trauma (Anderson and Spain, 1977; Skipper and Leonard, 1968).

A major problem with visiting children with disablement in hospital is arranging transport. Thus Baldwin (1975b) has reported that 58 per cent of parents in her Family Fund sample had difficulties in visiting their children or staying with them and Rutter *et al.* (1970b) found that 34 per cent of their sample had difficulties of some kind with transport. Major sources of complaint were that using public transport is very time-consuming (Rutter *et al.*, 1970b) and is sometimes expensive (McMichael, 1971). McMichael (*ibid.*) also discusses another problem – that many mothers find it difficult to visit their children because of their own ill-health or because they have no one to mind other children while they are away.

When hospital transport is available it has sometimes been refused on the grounds that the child falls outside the recognized categories of medical need or lives outside the normal service area (Baldwin, 1975b). The route taken by this transport is often circuitous and time-consuming and Baldwin reports that parents are never sure when, or indeed if, the transport is going to arrive. She summarizes her argument in these words:

> It is difficult to avoid concluding from the experience of both of the Family Fund and of our follow-up survey that many Area Health Authorities provide transport to hospital which is quite inadequate for the needs of severely handicapped children (*op.cit.*, p. 12).

Cost of transport to hospital

Burton (1975) found that 73 per cent of her sample of children with cystic fibrosis required regular transport to hospital. She attempted to assess the costs of providing this transport on an annual basis but, the research produced figures which varied widely. By comparison, Harrison's (1977) estimate that the costs of visiting for the parents of children hospitalized with Perthes' disease could reach £5 per week seems more meaningful.

Reports by Browse (1972, 1973) of work sponsored by the National Association for the Welfare of Children in Hospital have described current practice in providing assistance with the cost of visiting children in hospital with disablement. As far as can be estimated from the figures given, the costs per week of visiting such a child in 1971 were comparable to the £5 suggested by Harrison in 1977.

There is little definite evidence on the cost of transport to families with a child with disablement generally, though Butler *et al.* (1978) report that 43 per cent of their sample said that they experience financial hardship as a result of taking their child for outings and this may be as close as research can get to the problem.

Leisure

Lack of mobility, enuresis or behavioural disturbances obviously affects both outings and holidays (McMichael, 1971; Butler *et al.*, 1978), and in about 20 per cent of Rutter *et al.*'s (1970b) sample these disablements placed restrictions on family entertainment.

Hewett (1970) studied holidays among families containing a child with cerebral palsy and reported that 71 per cent of these families went on holiday and that most of them did not need to make special arrangements. At the same time their holiday experiences led many parents to think in terms of accepting special holidays for the child in the future.

Cull (1974) reported that 28 per cent of her sample of children with cystic fibrosis felt that their leisure activities were restricted by the cost of the child's disablement. Among the cœliac children studied as a control group, however, cost did not have as much effect on family outings and holidays as did the special diet required.

The extent of restriction obviously varies, the most important influences being the particular medical condition and the nature of the resulting impairments and disabilities. Families containing intellectually or multiply impaired children were especially restricted (Butler *et al.*, 1978), Woodburn (SB: 1973), Gregory (hearing impaired: 1976), Anderson and Spain (SB: 1977) all provide evidence of restrictions on leisure among particular groups of families.

Many researchers mention that children with disablement need a special kind of babysitter (Hewett, 1970; Fox, 1971; Moss and Silver, 1972; Baldwin, 1976; Lloyd-Bostock, 1976; Anderson and Spain, 1977; Harrison, 1977; Butler *et al.*, 1978). Hence services which provide trained sitters may be of considerable assistance to many parents (Heuston *et al.*, 1976).

Employment

A number of studies support the view that mothers of children with disablement are much less likely to work than are mothers generally (Woodburn, 1973; Baldwin, 1975; Butler *et al.*, 1976, 1978). Cull's study (1974) and that of Bradshaw (1978b) suggest that mothers of cystic fibrosis and incontinent children respectively were more likely to work, if at all, in the evenings or at night, presumably when fathers are at home.

Baldwin (1977) shows that if all mothers of disabled children who wished to work did so, then the proportion working would be greater than that in the general population. Baldwin infers from this that there may be a genuinely greater need for employment among these mothers, either because they need the money or because they want the company of others that work can provide. The evidence of Butler *et al.* (1978) seems to support the former reason. Though the findings of Woodburn (SB: 1973) and Harrison (CF: 1977) supports the latter reason, they relate only to mothers of children with particular disorders. Disablement in a child not only reduces the proportion of mothers who work, it also creates problems for those who do so (Burton, CF: 1975; Baldwin, 1977). Moss and Silver (1972) describe these problems as they apply to mothers of children with intellectual impairments.

There are fewer data on the employment problems of fathers of children with disablement, though Baldwin (1977) has estimated that about 25 per cent of fathers are affected adversely. She also describes several ways in which some fathers seek to compensate. Hunt (1976) reports fathers of children with spina bifida as changing jobs and careers in order to be more available at home.

Incontinence

Butler *et al.* (1978) show that incontinence is a very common impairment and Baldwin (1976) and Bradshaw (1978b) observe that incontinence was the second most common problem reported by families applying to the Family Fund. More detailed evidence of incontinence resulting from various medical conditions confirms how often their child's incontinence is the major problem facing parents of children with disabilities (Hewett, CP: 1970; Woodburn, SB: 1973;

Anderson and Spain, SB: 1977).

Bradshaw (1978b) has calculated that about 74 per cent of a sample of Family Fund applicants had incontinent children. He has analysed the factors associated with the incidence and degree of incontinence and has found that the major one was the medical condition. Bradshaw's main findings were that:

i.   severe incontinence was associated with spina bifida and/or hydrocephalus, microcephalus and other CNS malformations and tumours;

ii. moderate incontinence was associated with cerebral palsy, severe mental retardation and epilepsy;

iii. mild incontinence was associated with Down's syndrome, rubella syndrome, amputations, autism, deafness and blindness;

iv. *not* associated with incontinence were cystic fibrosis, hæmophilia, arthrogryphosis, Friedrich's ataxia, blood disorders and other physical malformations.

Bradshaw also showed that:

i.   age is related to the incidence of incontinence but not to its severity;

ii. mothers of incontinent children were less likely to work and, if they worked, were more likely to work part-time;

iii. children are less likely to be incontinent and less severely incontinent where there is an accessible indoor flush toilet. Where parents believed that their house was rendered unsuitable by reason of the child's impairment or disability they were more likely to have an incontinent child and the incontinence was likely to be more severe.

Evidence from Butler *et al.* (1978) shows that incontinence involved additional expense (85 per cent) or extra washing (98 per cent) on the part of parents. Bradshaw (1978b) gives the most detailed breakdown of costs. It seems that, at that time, weekly expenditure reported as directly attributable to the incontinence was £1.34. Bradshaw suggests that this figure is probably an underestimate because of the hidden costs of electricity for washing machines, wear and tear on clothes and machinery from very frequent washing, and the cost of maintaining a high level of hygiene when faced with incontinence. Bradshaw (1978b) is, in fact, very sceptical regarding the effectiveness of local authority incontinence services. He writes:

> While our earlier study on the consumers of the incontinence services left us with a sense of disbelief that the services could really be so inaccessible, limited in choice and under-used as the evidence suggested, this study has left us with a scepticism of the views of the authorities on the adequacy of their own services (*op.cit.*, p. 15).

Financial costs

The most detailed study of the cost of clothing, bedding and footwear is again that of the Family Fund team (Bradshaw, 1975; Baldwin, 1977); Bradshaw found that 40 per cent of applications to the Family Fund related to those areas of expenditure. In a sample of applicants to the Fund, 85 per cent had some needs for extra or special clothing as a result of the medical condition, though not all of them had actually applied for help with costs. Costs were related to the actual disorder. The highest proportion with extra clothing expenses were drawn mainly from children with epilepsy, mental retardation, cerebral palsy and spina bifida, in descending order. Mental and physical impairment together were more likely to involve extra costs than where the child was impaired in only one of these dimensions. The cost of providing extra clothing ranged from as little as £5 to as much as £150 per annum.

Baldwin (1977) investigated the cost of feeding children with disablement and reported that a fifth of families said that their child was more expensive to feed than normal. These were drawn mainly from:

i. those whose children had difficulty in swallowing, chewing or digesting food (cerebral palsy; severe mental retardation);

ii. those whose children needed special diets (diabetes; cœliac disease; phenylketonurea; kidney disease; spina bifida);

iii. those who undertook compensatory spending.

According to Baldwin, extra food costs ranged from a token sum to over £5 per week; the average being £1.83. Generally, the younger and more helpless the child and the smaller its intellectual capacity, the greater the expenditure. Extra costs for damage to furniture and fittings and more especially those arising from the need for extra heating are mentioned in several studies (Woodburn, SB: 1973; Baldwin, 1975, 1977; Burton, CF: 1975; Bradshaw, 1977). There is also evidence of extra expense arising from the provision of aids and appliances (Baldwin, 1977; Butler *et al.*, 1978).

Estimates of the proportion of families with disabled children who suffer hardship or financial difficulty because of the extra financial costs incurred by disablement vary considerably. In her study of children with cystic fibrosis, Burton (1975) found that, on average, families spent £39 per annum extra, with a variation from nothing to £250. Inevitably, expenditure varies according to the nature of the disorder or impairment and the severity of the resulting disabilities. Much of the evidence comes from samples of children suffering from spina bifida (Walker *et al.*, 1971; Richards and McIntosh, 1973; Woodburn, 1973), though evidence relating to children with cerebral palsy is provided by Hewett (1970). Information from one particular locality is provided by Jackson *et al.*, (1973), but again the most comprehensive and up-to-date information has come from the Family Fund (1975) researches. The major findings from Family Fund samples are summarized thus:

> The average amount spent in a year (on extra food, special diets, incontinence equipment, extra washing, extra clothes and bedding) . . . for the whole sample, including the 10 per cent with no extra expenditure (was) £107.15. . . . Just over a third of the sample spent between £10 and £75 a year and just over half between £76 and £200 (Baldwin, 1977, p. 28).

> Apart from poverty, which prevents need being translated into spending, and adequate services which can make (spending) less necessary, the most important factor in determining . . . extra costs . . . is the number and severity of the handicaps [WHO disabilities] the child has (*ibid.*, p. 29).

In addition, Bradshaw (1977) has reported that 45 per cent of the families in the Family Fund follow-up survey had net disposable resources of less than 40 per cent above supplementary benefit level. He and his team have also investigated the eligibility of Family Fund applicants for Social Security and other financial benefits such as the Attendance Allowance, the Mobility Allowance and those provided by local authorities. This matter is discussed on pp. 79–80 and 86–9.

ER THREE
ıcial and Emotional Problems of Parents of Children with Disablement

Introduction

In the preceding chapter, the literature relating to the practical and financial aspects of the problems faced by children with disablement and their families was considered. Problems of the kind discussed in that chapter largely impinge on the family as a whole. In the next four chapters, the literature on the social and emotional problems of these children and their families is reviewed. These problems are considered separately for the children themselves, their parents and their siblings. The reason for this approach is that though the literature shows that there is a real sense in which families as a whole are, for instance, isolated, it is mainly the parents, particularly the mother, who bears the major burden of isolation, certainly in the child's early years and perhaps later too. Further, the 'isolation' that is felt by the parents and the child himself or herself are in many ways different in nature and are treated in the literature as such. In this chapter the literature relating to the parents of the child with disablement is discussed, beginning with a consideration of their isolation in the community.

Isolation

Two general statements made by Kew (1975) and Spain (SB: 1973) respectively are that parents often become isolated from the community by caring for a child with disablement and that social isolation is greatest when the child is cared for within a single-parent family or when there is strain on the marital relationship.

These hardly unexpected findings are supplemented by a few more detailed studies of families with cystic fibrosis. On the basis of a small-scale study, Harrison (1977) reports that three out of the 12 families she studied had inflicted almost total isolation on themselves. The reasons they gave showed that this was their way of 'defending' themselves, though their own explanation was that they were afraid of leaving the child with others. Cystic fibrosis, because of its poor prognosis, may well make parents feel this way.

Burton's Scottish survey (1975) contains the finding that 26 per cent of mothers and 11 per cent of fathers felt isolated because of a general ignorance of cystic fibrosis in the community, while Cull's similar survey (1974) in Northern Ireland shows that the isolation is worst during the onset of symptoms and around the time of diagnosis. It may be that symptoms which give the child an appearance of looking distraught and neglected produces hostility in others and it is this hostility which results in the isolation of the parents. Diagnosis, at least when it is understood and accepted by the community, may serve to vindicate them.

Different parents will, of course, react differently under similar pressures. Hewett (CP: 1970) reports that 21 per cent of her sample of mothers felt lonely, but that some who appeared to have ample social contact felt lonely and some without them did not. Hence, she concluded 'that feelings of isolation were much more a function of the mother's personality, than of the presence of a handicapped child'.

Findings regarding the degree of isolation experienced and its ætiology vary considerably with the disease and aspect of isolation studied. For example, Woodburn (SB: 1973) reports that while a third of her sample of mothers felt that the child's disablement limited social contacts, 14 per cent felt that it actually increased them. However, both Woodburn (*op.cit.*), and Baldwin (1977) from a broader sample, highlight that loss of social contact which results from the mothers' not being able to work. Moroney (1976) suggests that mothers with intellectually impaired children are particularly isolated, though Rutter *et al.* (1970b) found that disruption in social relationships was only marginally more common for parents of these children than for those with physical impairments. Further, it seems that the overall hostility from relations or the general public to parents with such children is small (Rutter *et al.*, 1970b).

There is, however, still some evidence that particular groups of parents may suffer isolation disproportionately. Butler *et al.* (1976) found that mothers of children with disablement often had reduced contact when the disablement was severe, and Moss and Silver (1972) observed that some parents of children with intellectual impairments were isolated because neighbours did not understand the problems caused by these mental impairments. However, Walker *et al.* (1971) report that the interest of neighbours in children with spina bifida can be mere curiosity.

Stigma

There is a good deal of evidence that parents of children with disablement are disavantaged because of the impact of dominant cultural attitudes towards disablement and deviance generally. These problems have been extensively explored by several sociologists, Goffman's work (1963) being particularly well known. He suggests that the disabled in society are subject to a stigmatizing reaction from 'normal' others. However, those in close relationship with a person with disablement – termed 'wise' by Goffman – are also subject to stigma. Goffman writes about a particular kind of wise person in these terms:

> A second type of wise person is the individual who is related through the social structure to a stigmatised individual – a relationship that leads the wider society to treat both individuals in some respect as one . . . the parent of the cripple . . . (is) obliged to share some of the discredit of the stigmatised person to whom they are related.

Birenbaum's (1970) shorthand term for this experience is 'courtesy' stigma. People who bear this stigma are described by him as both 'normal' and 'different'. He expands his description thus: 'Their normality is obvious in their performance of conventional social roles; their differentness is occasionally manifested by their association with the stigmatised during encounters with normals . . .' (*op.cit.*, p. 196). Following Goffman, Birenbaum constructs three types of response possible to bearers of the courtesy stigma. They may (i) over-identify with the stigmatized, (ii) deny all association with them, or (iii) attempt a careful balance between the world of the stigmatized and that of the normal. This last-mentioned strategy particularly interests Birenbaum. Essentially, he is referring to what Goffman called 'passing', though he renames it 'consideration'. 'Consideration' is achieved through a mutual recognition of the child's disablement by the parent and his or her social contacts and by subsequent inattention to the stigma by both of them through a pact of tactful acceptance. Birenbaum describes consideration as meaning:

> . . . that the situation will never be spoken about unless brought up by the parents of the retarded child. Furthermore, comparisons between normal and retarded children will be carefully avoided . . . it means that friends will anticipate, and thereby avoid, any situation that might result in awkwardness or embarrassment for both . . . (*ibid.*, p. 199).

Birenbaum found that when 'consideration' was not shown, as when friends were condescending, relationships drifted apart. He also suggests that mothers will make sacrifices for the child only so far as this does not affect the 'normal-appearing round of life'. Unfortunately, the problems faced in fulfilling social roles can produce a withdrawal of consideration. As a result the bearer of the courtesy stigma will often be forced to have recourse to one or other of the more extreme responses to stigma.

Voysey (1975) criticizes Birenbaum's analysis as being of too limited applicability. She argues that we need to consider the parent as someone who has no choice but to take on a courtesy stigma. What is more, far from being expected to reject or limit association with the stigmatized, the parent is encouraged to welcome its responsibilities. Hence she suggests that we need to: '. . . examine the conditions under which parents adopt different methods of managing interaction with others in such a way that, far from avoiding interaction, they may become more than normally competent performers' (*op.cit.*, p. 130). For Voysey, therefore, parents are involved in constantly attempting to create and maintain an impression of conventional parenthood. They negotiate with others over the recognition and definition of the disablement, its severity, visibility, etc. They monitor and channel information about the child so as to elicit support and avoid embarrassment, and they attempt to obtain information from others so as to inform their activity as impression managers. From this perspective, statements made by parents of children with disablement are seen as part of the process of constructing, as far as possible, a normal identity for the family.

Voysey describes the strategies which parents adopt along two axes – responsibility and power, i.e. whether they are seen by others as responsible for a child's condition and whether they have power to ameliorate it. Thus the 'not responsible/have power' strategy will result in a style of 'coping splendidly'; a style widely legitimated by formal and informal caring agencies. The other presentations are:

i.   'responsible/have power': 'making amends'. This involves visible special efforts and sacrifices on behalf of the child.
ii. not responsible/no power: 'stoic acceptance', 'facing the facts'.
iii. responsible/no power: similar to the response described by Birenbaum, involves avoiding encounters.

In general, Voysey's conceptualization, of which the above is but a brief and incomplete summary, offers us a means of understanding why the findings of studies involving the parents of children whose disablement is of different forms vary so much. We cannot consider families with such children apart from their social existence in which they negotiate their identity. So Voysey reminds us that, because of the inevitably social nature of disablement, even apparently sound empirical research into its concomitants will inevitably result in apparently contradictory findings which are difficult to interpret without more attention to the social processes involved.

Marital problems

The proportion of parents of children with disablement who become divorced shows considerable variation between studies. The differences could well be related to the methodology employed and Stevenson *et al.* (1977) have discussed some of the problems of assessing the proportion of parents who become divorced. Their own estimate, which is based on the work of Tew *et al.* (1977), was that the rate of divorce among families with children with spina bifida is, at most, 1.5 times that of the general population. In general, where controls have been used, significant differences are not found (Martin, SB: 1975; Gath, DS: 1977).

Data on the influence of a child with disablement on marital relationships generally, also leads to conflicting conclusions. For example, Gath (*ibid.*), who is one of the few researchers who has tried to use objective measures of parental relationships, reports that the sample scored more highly on the negative measures of marital relations than did controls, but that they also scored more highly on the positive measures. Most researchers in this area do not go much beyond suggesting the identity of intervening variables between the presence of a child with disablement and the existence of marital problems. Examples of the variables suggested are mental instability (Dorner, SB: 1973); sexual difficulties (Emery *et al.*, MD: 1973; Kew, 1975); fear of further pregnancies (McMichael, 1971; Cull, CF: 1974; Burton, CF: 1975); previous marital strain (Martin, 1975); physical and emotional fatigue (Cull, CF: 1974), and the husband in unskilled work (Gibson, 1974).

Tew (1974), Tew and Laurence (1976) and Tew *et al.* (1977) suggest that the birth of a child with spina bifida initially unites the parents, but subsequently leads to increased strain and an above-average rate of breakdown, while Kolin *et al.* (1971) suggest that the stability of the marriage as indicated by its duration indicates good possibilities of resisting breakdown: '. . . only parents who had the opportunity to develop a stable relationship over a minimum of five years of marriage were able to cope successfully with the crisis presented by the defective child'.

Martin's evidence (1975) is much less clear-cut and, in part, contradicts this finding. He found that where parents perceived the child's disablement as resulting in considerable stress and where there were also previous marital problems then there was likely to be marital breakdown. Of those of his sample who separated, 75 per cent reported marital strain prior to the child's birth. He found no evidence to support the view that marriages of over five years duration with at least one normal child and where the affected child was planned were less likely to experience breakdown.

Burton (CF: 1975) cites evidence that marital strain is related to four main factors:

i. the experience of guilt when the condition has a genetic basis,

ii.   the existence of an unsatisfactory relationship with the spouse,
iii.   the fear of another pregnancy,e pregnancy,
iv.   the experience of having lost previous children.

Several writers suggest that basic incompatibility between the parents is by far the most important factor in marital breakdown among parents of a child born with impairments (Hewett, CP: 1970; Spain, SB: 1973; Dorner, SB: 1975; Martin, SB: 1975). However, there is so much conflicting evidence that only studies based on examining both 'structural' factors (the age of the parents at marriage, their social class, their income, family structure) and personal factors (expectations that parents have of their marriage, perception of their responsibilities towards the child) are likely to provide definitive answers.

Single parenthood

Estimates of the proportion of children with disablement in one-parent households vary from about one in twelve (Woodburn, SB: 1973) to one in seven (Hitch, 1974). The general survey of Butler *et al.* (1978) suggest a proportion of about one in ten, the same as that suggested by the General Household Survey.

Many of these children are likely to have their handicaps exacerbated by being brought up by a single parent. Spain (1973) found evidence of greater social isolation and Ouston (1973) has noted, not surprisingly, that single parents with a child with disablement have lower income and greater difficulties with housing than the average parent.

Stress

Obviously, the presence of a child with disablement in a family produces demands on family members. In time, fulfilling these demands produces 'stress'.

This simple formulation is elaborated by Harrison (1977) and Bradshaw and Lawton (1978) who describe the production of stress in terms of a model which can be represented roughly as in Figure 2.

**Figure 2: Model of how a child with disablement produces stress
in the parents**

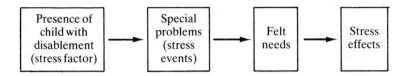

Examples of the 'special problems' within the model are physical
and emotional strain, transport difficulties, etc. Examples of 'felt
needs' are those for money, support and information, while the
'stress effect' is defined in terms of physical, emotional and financial
consequences. Bradshaw (*op.cit.*) lists these stress effects in three
categories: (i) physical burdens of care, (ii) financial strain, and
(iii) emotional and psychosomatic symptoms. Of these the third is
most often discussed in research, though several studies also report
on the general 'health' of parents, especially mothers. These latter
reports vary widely in their conclusions, though most (e.g. McAndrew, 1976; McMichael, 1971; Roskies, Th: 1972) suggest a high
prevalence or incidence of problems. The only study employing a
control, that of Gath (1977), suggests that long-term health problems do not occur among mothers caring for a child with disablement any more than they do among mothers generally. However,
Burton (CF: 1975) reports that 87 per cent of fathers and 60 per cent
of mothers in her sample exhibited symptoms such as feeling ill or
depression on hearing the news of their child's impairment.

Generally, the evidence on stress effects relates to the borderline
area of physical/emotional problems. Thus Butler *et al.* (1978)
asked a broad sample of mothers of a child with disablement
whether they had experienced certain types of symptoms in the
month before interview. The responses to the questionnaire are
shown in Table 2.

More symptoms were reported than among those in a comparable
group whose stress was brought on by moving house. However,
Butler *et al.* (*ibid.*) point out that the house survey took place seven
years earlier and suggest that over the seven years the tendency to
report or experience stress may have increased in the general population.

Butler *et al.* (*ibid.*) also used the Morbid Anxiety Inventory in
their survey. This inventory is generally recognized as a reasonably

Table 2: Reported symptoms of mothers (percentages)

Symptom	Per cent without symptoms	Per cent with symptoms	
		Doctor not seen	Doctor seen
Headaches	33	43	24
Sleeplessness	60	23	17
Stomach or bowel upset	79	11	10
Sweating	73	19	8
Nerves	48	23	27
Depression	54	25	21

well-validated rating scale. They found that the results using this scale did not differ much from those obtained by a straightforward questionnaire to elicit symptoms so they did not proceed far with their analysis of the results. From the results of a 'fatalism' scale which they did analyse they put forward the suggestion that subjects experience anxiety when they feel that events are outside their control. Hence anxiety and stress may be associated with feelings of helplessness (i.e. fatalism) in relation to the child with disablement.

Other studies report that a high proportion of mothers show signs of stress (Dormer, SB: 1973; Hewett, SB: 1970; Cull, CF: 1974; McMichael, CP: 1971; Walker *et al.*, SB: 1971, Richards and McIntosh, SB: 1973). Some of these studies concentrate on mothers with children suffering from one particular condition so that findings are often based on rather small samples. Cull's survey data are better than most though confined to mothers of children with cystic fibrosis. She found that 79 per cent of these mothers complained of sleeplessness, 86 per cent felt run down or depressed and 57 per cent felt nervous. Cull administered a 'Manifest Anxiety Scale' (Taylor 1953) and recorded a mean score for fathers of 14.8 and for mothers of 22.4 (the norm for young adults is 14.5). Baldwin (1976) confirms the impression conveyed by Cull's results in a sample of parents drawn from a wider base. She reports that only 22 per cent of mothers and 50 per cent of fathers in her sample felt that their physical or mental health had *not* been affected.

A cautionary note is sounded by a carefully controlled study of Hare *et al.* (1972). In a study of a group of mothers of young children with spina bifida (n = 90), a control group of mothers (n = 76) who had had normal babies was set up. It was found that there was no marked difference between the two groups in the number of symptoms recorded nor in their mean scores on the Manifest Personality Inventory (MPI), though mothers in both groups with high N (neuroticism) scores reported more symptoms.

Several studies have used a 'Malaise Inventory' developed from the Cornell Medical Index (Brodman *et al.*, 1949, 1952) to detect emotional disturbance. This scale has been validated by Rawnsley (1966) and by Gibson *et al.* (1967) who have demonstrated substantial agreement between the scale and independent psychiatric assessment. Rutter *et al.* (1970a, 1970b) have made extensive use of a version of the scale and have reached the following conclusions:

i.   Generally insignificant differences between mothers (n = 160) of neurologically impaired children and comparable controls, except for mothers of children with epilepsy (1970a, pp. 160–1).

ii. Mothers of children suffering from a psychiatric disorder scored consistently higher than mothers of children with physical impairment (1970b).

iii. Mothers who perceived their child's impairment as having a considerable effect on family life were likely to report more symptoms of malaise in themselves (1970a, p. 160).

iv. Severe physical impairment in the child was associated with the malaise score only in a few cases (1970a, p. 161).

v.   High malaise scores are associated with maternal ill-health lasting at least one month in the year previous to interview (1970b, p. 343).

vi. Mothers of children with diagnosed psychiatric disorder admitted to more symptoms than mothers of children with other impairments (1970b, pp. 340–1).

The Malaise Inventory has been used in several other studies. The results usually indicate some relationship between malaise in mothers and impairment in the children, though the evidence is not uniform. Thus Moss and Silver (1972), not using controls, found that 40 per cent of mothers of children with mental retardation attending a Liverpool special school were 'emotionally disturbed'. However, Gath (1977) found no significant difference between parents of children with Down's syndrome and controls. Also using controls, Tew and Laurence (SB: 1976) found substantial differences in the mean scores of mothers of children with spina bifida aged eight to ten who were under stress because of overnight stays in hospital. The SB mothers' mean score was 7.1, that of the control was 4.7. In another paper Tew and Laurence (1975) report significantly higher scores in the malaise scores of (i) mothers of children in special schools compared with mothers of children in ordinary schools, (ii) mothers of incontinent children compared with mothers of continent children, (iii) mothers of children with IQ < 80 compared with mothers of children with IQ > 80. Tew and Laurence's findings therefore suggest a positive relationship between degree of disablement and malaise.

Finally, Bradshaw and Lawton (1978) administered the malaise scale to 303 mothers of children with severe disablement who therefore met the requirements for help from the Family Fund. Their findings were that the level of stress was determined primarily by 'internal' factors such as the physiology and 'personality' of the mother. They concluded that these factors were not affected in any specific way by the 'external' social and physical conditions of the family and the child.

Certain possible special antecedents of stress are considered by Fotheringham and Creal (1974) and by Linde *et al.* (1970). The former refer to the effects of the form and nature of the impairment on the physical appearance of the child; the latter emphasizes the effect of the 'visibility' of the impairment.

Taking all studies together, there is reasonably firm evidence that the parents of children with disablement are more likely than parents of children without disablement to suffer from stress, anxiety and depression. The factors involved are, however, complex so that only the more carefully controlled studies using validated instruments and methodologies produce reliable findings on the identity and mechanism of these factors. Further, as the next chapter will show, many of the more recent studies are now tending to extend beyond the mere diagnosis of the factors producing problems or the form that problems take to studying *how* families might best cope with and adapt to disablement.

CHAPTER FOUR
Parental Adaptation and Coping

Introduction

On the whole, this chapter will concentrate on the problem of defining terms such as adaptation and coping in such a way that researches undertaken from different perspectives can be compared. It also contains some mention of the problems which can arise because professionals often appear to have difficulty in understanding the perspectives of parents. This matter will receive fuller discussion in the final chapter, though we would mention here one approach – that of Voysey (1975) – which seems to throw light on this particular issue. She has looked at the processes by which parents construct for themselves the 'meaning' of the child's disablement through 'commonsense' explanations. She attempts to do this by establishing the contexts in which parents negotiate with society at large for such meanings and by showing how different contexts constrain parents to produce different meanings. She shows, for instance, how parents' initial reaction to the child's impairment and the style of their subsequent coping will both be influenced by the way in which they normalize discrepancies between actual and expected events in their experience of rearing the child. It seems that the clarity of the diagnosis and the way in which parents are informed of it is a particularly vital factor in their subsequent coping.

Work from a similar perspective is that of Jaehnig (1974, 1975). He also emphasizes the importance of parents' perceptions of disablement, suggesting that 'The point of perceptions is that they constitute an attempt by parents to construct a meaning from something they never anticipated' (1975, p. 85). Jaehnig give examples of a variety of styles of coping which illustrate the interrelationship between personal perceptions and coping. If this approach is followed, the key to adaptation and coping appears to be the parents' ability to 'normalize' their child (Hewett, 1970). Roskies (1972) has suggested that this ability in mothers is manifested where they are able to maintain habitual or expected child-rearing practices and customary values and goals (*op.cit.*, p. 235).

Scope and approach of the research

Most of the research concentrates on describing the personal and psychological responses of parents to the birth of a child with impairments. There is less consideration of how the form those responses take is conditioned by social and cultural factors. Thus MacKeith (1973) has suggested that the birth of a child with impairments raises complexes of 'feelings' in the parents. These include 'biological' reactions, such as the wish to protect the helpless, or a revulsion at the abnormal. They may also include 'inadequacy' as a reproducer of the species and as a child-bearer, and a sense of bereavement which progresses through anger and grief before adjustment takes place. Each of these complexes will have behavioural reciprocals: over-protection, rejection, depression, aggression, disbelief, withdrawal, adaptation. Gould (1968), Fox (1977), Tew (1974), Kew (1975), Burton (1975) and Rutter *et al.* (1970b) put forward similar descriptions of parental response but with minor variations.

Another description is provided by Bentovim (1972) who writes of the birth as a period of 'intense crisis' in which the parents experience numbness, grief, disgust, waves of helplessness, rage and disbelief. He suggests that parents may experience a wish to get rid of the child and in consequence may suffer guilt, self-blame, shame and anxiety which in the mother are sufficient to disturb normal maternal feelings. Bowley (1967) and Sheridan (1965) refer to four likely reactions to these feelings: acceptance, over-protection, over-pressure and rejection, the first two being the most common.

Perhaps the most useful descriptions of parental response are those which conceptualize stages of adaptation by which parents come to terms with the birth of a child with impairments. Mattson (1972) describes three such stages: (i) acute anxiety and fears of the death of the child, (ii) denial of the existence or extent of the impairment, a phase in which they seek out more advice and (iii) acceptance. Richmond (1973) has a simpler conceptualization within which he uses the terms disorganization, reintegration and adaptation to describe the same three stages. Finally, Drotar *et al.* (1975) have developed a five-stage model of parental response on the basis of a small-scale study. The stages are (i) shock, (ii) denial, (iii) sadness, (iv) anxiety and anger and (v) adaptation.

In all the studies mentioned above there is a tendency to view the birth of a child with impairments as a 'disaster'. Other studies, describing the factors which influence the nature and intensity of the parental response and their degree of adaptation qualify this tendency somewhat. Thus Jobling (1975) suggests that parents react better if the impairment is discovered when the child is young. Similarly, Steinhauer (1974) argues that the age of onset and diagnosis, as well as severity and prognosis, will affect adaptation. Goddard and Rubissow (1977) suggest that the shock is greater and recovery is slower when it is the first child who is born with impairments.

The description of reaction and adaptation in terms of a time sequence is another characteristic of most of the descriptions of parental response to the birth of a child with impairments. This approach promotes an expectation that parents will eventually turn from exhibiting grief to caring for the child. Whether this expectation is really well-founded is occasionally questioned (Martin, 1975). Certainly Gath (1977) found that 90 per cent of parents of children with Down's syndrome still expressed grief over the birth of the child six years later. It may be that parental reactions do not always 'develop' through time-defined stages. This issue will be touched on again in the remaining sections of this chapter.

Methods of adaptation

As a general rule, within the literature on parental adaptation to the child, personal and psychological variables are concentrated on to the neglect of social and cultural variables. The consequence of this approach, in the words of Birch (1964), has been '. . . to narrow the range of definition of family effects so as to implicate essentially personality and psychological processes within the family unit' (*op.cit.*, p. 86). One practical issue which is considered by several writers is the separation of mother and child at birth. It seems clear that at birth the medical need for prolonged separation of mother and child can cause problems (Walker *et al.*, SB: 1971; Woodburn, SB: 1973; Hunt, SB: 1976). However, Roskies (Th: 1972) suggests that separation may actually help some mothers to stabilize. Whichever view is correct, there seems no doubt that attempts to involve mothers while the child is receiving hospital care are essential (Brimblecombe, 1974). Nevertheless, very strenuous attempts to involve the mother could carry with them the assumption that parents will invariably accept and care for the child however serious its disablement.

Kolin *et al.*'s work (1971) is a good example of the tendency to consider mainly personal and psychological variables affecting parental adaptation to a child with impairments. They refer to parents as mobilizing a series of 'defence mechanisms' in order to adapt to and accept the child. Poorly-adjusted parents tended to use projection, rejection, over-protection and denial; the well-adapted parents utilized a wish for another child and religion. Sheridan (1965) and Bowley (1967) provide similar accounts of adaptation.

The writers who challenge this approach question particularly how realistic are societal expectations of 'acceptance'. They refer to, for instance, conflict between acceptance of the unacceptable and rejection of the real (Fox, 1977). Roskies (Th: 1972) quotes a parent: 'As a member of a community you must recognise your child as a deviant – as a mother you must love it' (*op.cit.*, p. 97). Similarly, in a study of children with intellectual impairments, Jaehnig (1974) regards 'acceptance' as part of an arsenal of concepts which professionals are prone to use when they sit in judgment on the family. He suggests that acceptance often '. . . bears a symbolic importance, representing superior knowledge possessed by the professional worker, while belittling parents' attempts to make sense of the situation' (*op.cit.*, p. 61). In fact, Jaehnig feels that parents are put into a 'double bind' in which they can do not right:

'. . . if parents keep the child at home they endanger their mental stability or the development of other children; if they seek residential care they are rejecting the child; if they try to stimulate him, they fail to accept the reality of the handicap; if they cater to his whims they contribute to his dependence. . . . they have no description of acceptable behaviour and any action they take puts them in the position of needing the social worker's ministrations (*ibid.*, p. 77).

As is mentioned above, several researchers have described the 'defence mechanisms' which parents use in order to adapt to the child. Other researchers concentrate on investigating the incidence of particular mechanisms. Since total abandonment is quite rare (Spain, SB: 1973; Richards and McIntosh, SB: 1973; Laurence, 1976), several writers describe degrees of parental *rejection*. Mc-Michael (1971) reports that 31 per cent of the mothers in her sample showed 'moderately severe' or 'severe' degrees of rejection of the child. In America, Arnold (1976) suggests that rejection as shown by battering and neglect may be more prevalent among children with disablement than among children without it. There is limited support for this proposition in British evidence. Smith and Hanson (1974) report that of a sample of 134 battered children admitted to hospital, ten suffered from 'a serious congenital defect'. However, evidence of this kind from a small sample without use of a control group inevitably leaves the position unclear.

Over-protection

A more common response than rejection to physical impairment in a child is *over-protection*. Poznanski (1973) suggests that it is 'highly common', being the result of parental denial of anger, resentment and guilt. However, more recent studies draw attention to the existence of different views of what counts as over-protection and consequent problems of definition. Also Hewett (1976) has suggested that earlier researchers often confused 'ordinary' and pathological behaviour. Oliver (1976) has reviewed the literature on over-protection and argues that in order to establish the existence of over-protection as a mode of behaviour one would need to demonstrate the existence of high degrees of frequency, intensity, duration and resistance to extinction of attachment and dependency behaviour in a mother-child relationship. He suggests that this has yet to be done in families with children without impairments. Yet, to establish what maternal and caretaker behaviours are unnecessary is obviously very problematic in 'normal' families. Further, we cannot define a child as 'abnormal' because he is impaired and then suggest that he is 'over-protected' because he is not treated like a normal child. As Jaehnig (1974) implies, the advice 'treat him like a normal child', so often proffered, is little more than a denial that problems exist. Jaehnig also suggests that those who proffer such advice seem likely to diagnose over-protection in parents.

A possible approach to solving the problem of deciding what is to count as over-protection is to compare the parents' treatment of the child with disablement with their treatment of the child's siblings. Using this approach, Cull (CF: 1974) found that most (Scottish) parents made some concessions to the child with disablement; 34 per cent of mothers and 43 per cent of fathers said they were less likely to punish the child and only 26 per cent of mothers and 32 per cent of fathers made no concessions. Cull's findings also show, however, that only 20 per cent of parents modify their expectations of the child at home and that 33 per cent of mothers and 22 per cent of fathers expected less of the child at school. Outside the home less independence was generally allowed and less was expected of the children in their activities.

In an equivalent study in Northern Ireland, Burton (CF: 1975) obtained comparable figures. She found that 53 per cent treated the child with disablement differently from siblings and that a further 18 per cent who denied treating the child differently were found after closer questioning to do so. Forty-six per cent were less likely to punish the child and many felt guilty or uncomfortable when they did.

Burton also observed that mothers changed expectations more than fathers, that parents from higher socioeconomic classes changed more than other parents, and that parents who had already lost a child expected much less of their child with disablement. Other interesting findings made by Burton were that parents of those children with disablement who were able to talk about their illness were those who changed expectations least, and that 44 per cent of parents were unhappy about their treatment of the child. Those who were happy were those who saw the child as 'different' and so felt that it was ridiculous to treat him or her as a 'normal' child.

Hewett (1970), researching families of children with cerebral palsy, found that about 72 per cent of parents said that their policy of smacking was the same for the child with disablement as for other siblings. She summarizes thus: 'It seems from this evidence that most mothers include their handicapped child in the family patterns of control as much as they can, but they do have to modify their approach to this area of child-rearing where the degree or kind of handicap dictates' (*op.cit.*, p. 94). Rutter *et al.*'s, (1970b) evidence is particularly useful because their sample was not confined to children with a particular disease or defect. They found that a third of their sample did not smack their child with disablement compared with only three per cent in a control group.

Another source of evidence on the existence of over-protection is that of parents sharing a room or bed with the child with disablement. Newson and Newson's (1968) broadly-based Nottingham sample of all children suggested that about 14 per cent shared their parents' room. In Hewett's (*op.cit.*) sample of children with cerebral palsy this percentage is doubled, though the reasons are often irrelevant to disablement *per se* – the age of the child and shortage of accommodation, for instance. Hewett concludes that when all factors were considered, there were only two children for whom sharing could not be attributed to 'reasonable' factors of this kind. Similarly, only five children in her sample shared their parents' bed and this practice was not unknown in the Nottingham sample. Hewett (*ibid.*) found, in fact, that mothers of children with cerebral palsy were *less* likely to take their child into bed with them if his or her sleep were disturbed than were mothers of children generally (40 per cent as against 66 per cent for Newson's sample). Finally, Burton (CF: 1975) found that 25 per cent of her sample shared their parents' room and though some shared because of lack of accommodation, she feels that sharing was most often arranged to meet emotional needs rather than practical necessity.

Overall, there does seem to be some modification in the expectations that parents have of their child with disablement. There are also corresponding adjustments to discipline. Whether or not these modifications and adjustments can be referred to as 'over-protection' is uncertain. Jaehnig's (1974) view is that parents tend to be judged abnormal by association. Hence as the remarks of Oliver (1976) and others cited on p. 41 suggest, a convincing test of hypotheses about parental over-protection and similar deviant behaviours would require studies using intensive observation and carefully selected controls.

Coping with the child

As with adaptation and over-protection, what counts as 'coping' is problematical. A multitude of responses is covered by concepts of this kind, varying from the parents coming to terms with the implications of the disablement to their defending themselves against negative social reactions. Kellmer Pringle and Fiddes (1970), however, interpret the evidence to suggest that extreme responses are typical: 'The evidence suggests that the presence of a severely handicapped child in a family produces one of two diametrically opposed and extreme situations: either the parents cope admirably . . . or the family proves unequal to the tremendous strain . . .' (*op.cit.*, p. 65). Cull (1974) and Burton (1975) surveying parents of children with cystic fibrosis would not agree. Both found much resentment and many feelings of discouragement among these parents. Cull constructed an index of parental coping from indicators such as extent of understanding of the diagnosis, meeting other responsibilities and avoiding anxiety and depression. She found that those who coped best tended to show least resentment of the sacrifices required. Burton (*op.cit.*) also found much resentment in her sample; it occurred in 36 per cent of mothers and 45 per cent of fathers.

Burton, Cull and several other writers discuss the factors influencing adaptation and acceptance. Cull (1974) and Shakespeare (1975) find that younger mothers have most difficulty in adapting; Tyler and Kogan (1977) mention that the unrewarding nature of the child's responses may lead to 'affect turn-off' in the mother, and Jobling (1975) and Burton (1975) find acceptance is easier when diagnosis occurs early in the child's life. It has also been suggested (by Goddard and Rubissow (1977)) that parents have most difficulty in accepting impairment when it occurs in the first child.

Among several factors preventing adjustment, McMichael (1971) mentions fears about the future. Indeed, there is considerable agreement among writers that most parents have major worries about the child's future. Thus, Burton (CF: 1975) found that 80 per cent of the mothers and 76 per cent of the fathers preferred not to think or plan for the future. Roskies (Th: 1972) and Minde *et al.* (1972) found the same tendency, though they do not cite exact figures. Eighty-three per cent of McAndrew's (1976) Australian sample said that their main worry was the child's future, and only four per cent of Butler *et al.*'s (1978) sample had no fears at all for the future. Nevertheless, Richards and McIntosh (SB: 1973) found most parents to be unrealistic about the future; as many as 60 out of the 72 who were prepared to answer the question said that they expected the child's condition to be cured or much relieved.

Family involvement in care

On the relative degree of participation by husband and wife in activities involving the child with disablement, it seems that only a minority of fathers are significantly involved (Baldwin, 1976). In a study of children who were mentally retarded, Wilkin (1978) concludes that only 25 per cent of fathers helped their wife to any real extent. Other researchers e.g. McAndrew (1976), in an Australian study, agree with the general trend of this finding, though Burton (CF: 1975) records that 27 per cent of fathers had had to give up work at some time to care for the child, while Cull (CF: 1974) found that fathers were more willing to help in caring than their actual recorded involvement of about three minutes a day would suggest.

A few studies examine the kind of help that fathers give or, more usually, do *not* give. For example, Anderson and Spain (SB: 1977) observed that few fathers could manage the child's urine bags and Walker *et al.* (SB: 1971) found that 35 per cent of fathers gave no help with bathing the baby, changing nappies or going shopping; 21 per cent gave help with one of these items and 18 per cent with two; twenty-one per cent gave assistance with all three tasks.

Hewett's study (1970) is useful because she used a control group of non-impaired children to study the participation of fathers in the care of their children with cerebral palsy. Her conclusion was that: 'There was no evidence to support the view that a high proportion of fathers of handicapped children are more involved with the children than would be "culturally expected", at least in the eyes of the mother' (*op.cit.*, p. 107).

Summary

In Chapters Three and Four of this study we have reviewed the literature on the problems of parents of a child with disablement and some of the ways in which they cope with these problems. As was implied at the end of Chapter Three, it seems that researchers in this area have begun to take an approach which asks *how* families manage to cope with, adapt to and accept disablement, rather than one which only investigates *why* some deviant families do not. In other words, research is now less judgmental, focussing less on the faults of individuals and more on ways in which families can be helped. However, it is clear from the literature that many families are not really coping, even though they are not breaking down. Rather they experience and meet their problems to the best of their abilities and often face secondary problems as a result. It is often the accumulation of these problems that disturbs relationships within the family and between the family and society. It is this disturbance which in turn brings the family into contact with professionals (Jaehnig, 1974, p. 179).

In brief, therefore, research is now beginning to demonstrate that the real problem is not so much one of family pathology as one of how to give practical assistance to families while, at the same time, keeping in mind that the tasks they face are so difficult that only a few exceptional families can be expected to be fully equipped to undertake them without help from outside.

CHAPTER FIVE

The Social and Emotional Problems of the Child with Disablement

Introduction

A common theme in the literature relating to children with disablement is that they are particularly susceptible to social and emotional problems associated directly or indirectly with their experience of diseases, disorders and disablement. In fact, the bulk of research activity has approached this theme from one particular standpoint only – exploring the child's adaptation to his experience. In following the literature, therefore, it is difficult to see how this will allow any kind of analysis of the child's experience of disablement from the standpoint of the ICIDH. Rather, we shall find that the literature describes the social and psychological factors and problems which *interact with* the child's impairments and disabilities to produce the residual limitations on the child's everyday life – his handicaps. We have to recognize, therefore, that the literature virtually starts where the ICIDH leaves off. The ICIDH provides us with a way of describing disablement more or less objectively; it does not appear to provide us with a way of describing how the child reacts to it. Nevertheless, as the work of Shakespeare (1975) described on p. 52 seems to imply, it could well provide an analysis of disablement which matches in complexity that which psychologists make of behavioural problems, so that the links between the experience and the behaviour can be explored more adequately than they have been in the past.

As a whole the literature emphasizes that most children born with impairments are likely to experience physical and emotional problems of some kind in the neo-natal period. It is suggested that these problems are linked to the mother's experience of early separation and her feelings of ambivalence following diagnosis; both of which affect her ability to care for the child. For instance, Kogan and Tyler (1973, 1976) suggest that mothers of children with disablement often experience 'affect turn-off' because of the unrewarding nature of interaction with the child which stems, in turn, from the child's failure to develop independence. Cashdan (1968) describes the phenomenon of affect turn-off in terms of less than normal affection and stimulation; Burton (1975) in terms of diminished self-confidence, while Fox (1977) argues that as the child grows he experiences his parents as incompetent compared with professionals. Both Cashdan (*op.cit.*) and Kogan and Tyler (*op.cit.*) also suggest that many parents are likely to expect too much, too soon. Consequently they become discouraged and 'give up' when the child does not respond.

Problems of adaptation

The theme of this chapter obviously links with those of the previous two. But the direct effect of the parental problems discussed in those chapters on the disabled child's development is not easy to disentangle from other influences. Hence researchers have generally contented themselves with straightforwardly describing the problems for the child in adapting and adjusting to chronic illness and disablement. Mattson (1972) has outlined three forms of poor adjustment: over-dependency, over-independency and isolation. The first of these is characterized by fearfulness and inactivity, with the child lacking friends and not participating in outside activities. Their mothers are themselves fearful and are over-protective. In the second, the child is over-independent, highly active and daring, engaging in risk-taking and prohibited activities. The third type of poor adjustment is found mostly among children with a congenital impairment. The child is shy and lonely and has feelings of resentment about his condition, seeing it as an injustice. Mattson (*op.cit.*) suggests that this is a response to parental shame and embarrassment.

Several researchers have made studies of the reactions to their experience of groups of children with particular diseases and disorders. Thus Meijer (1971) in a study of children with myelodyplastic disorders suggests that they feel that they have been punished and that this may be the basis of their hostile attitude to others. This hostility, he suggests, is introjected so that a masochistic attitude and self-disgust result. The impairment of these children's ability to manipulate and inspect objects may result in their becoming resigned and frustrated. Similarly, incontinence leads to feelings of self-blame and, for those who were hospitalized, there was evidence of depression and feelings of inferiority, inadequacy and deprivation.

Tinkelman *et al.* (1976) have studied children with chronic asthma who experienced repeated hospitalization. They found that during group therapy 'anger, guilt, fear and sadness surfaced repeatedly' (*op.cit.*, p. 176). The children were also found to have difficulties in expressing verbal anger to their parents and siblings and were envious of others' normality.

In these and similar psychotherapeutic or psychoanalytic studies, there is an obvious tendency to view impairment as an emotionally as well as a physically crippling event. The child is seen as having to accept his own unacceptability so that he will inevitably have severe emotional difficulties.

At a rather more mundane level of analysis there is some consensus that the restriction of movement experienced by many children with disablement lies behind many of their emotional difficulties. Rutter *et al.* (1970a, b) suggest that restriction of this kind can lead to feelings of being of little worth or to the child becoming hypochondriacal, while Bentovim (1972) argues that because these children are less able to explore their environment they are likely to find routine particularly comforting and that this may lead to overdependence on others. He also suggests that too much care or too perfect care means that failure, an essential component of childhood experience, does not occur.

There is firm evidence to support the view that the social skills of children with disablement are likely to be underdeveloped (Cannell III, 1970; McMichael, 1971; Anderson, 1973; Fulthorpe, SB: 1974). Other effects of disablement are suggested by Volpe (1976) who found that children with it often adopt a 'patient' (as opposed to an 'agent') role. Similarly, Richardson *et al.* (1964) obtained evidence consistent with a view that disablement in children results in lower levels of self-confidence and greater self-depreciation. Boys particularly reported difficulties in interpersonal relationships because of functional limitations and disabilities resulting from physical impairment. However, the degree to which disablement by itself is the main factor in producing deficiencies in social skills is not entirely clear, since there are both inevitable interactions between factors and many problems in validly testing social skills.

Emotional and behavioural problems

Younger children

It used to be believed that children with physical disablement are inevitably more likely to be disturbed than are children without such disablement. Since the publication of Pilling's (1972, 1973a, 1973b, 1973c, 1975) reviews of relevant research this view is less easily sustained. Pilling's syntheses suggest that, apart from children with cerebral palsy, psychiatric disorder is only slightly more prevalent among children with disablement than among the general population of children. More precisely, she suggests that the literature indicates that:

  i.   when physical impairment is associated with brain disorder there will be a higher prevalence of psychiatric disturbance,
  ii. there is no specific type of psychiatric disorder associated with physical disorders generally,
  iii. the highest prevalence of psychiatric disorder in children with a specific physical disorder occurs among those with cerebral palsy where there is a neurological involvement.

The best evidence comparing children with disorders of different kinds is to be found in the studies of Rutter *et al.* (1970a, b); Seidel *et al.* (1975) and Anderson (1973).

Several other studies contain relevant findings, usually from specific diagnostic categories of physical disorder. A persistent problem in comparing the results of different studies is not only that the children are put into different diagnostic categories, but that the types of behaviour resulting from disablement and/or disorder used as criteria vary quite widely. Even though, for instance, Kellmer Pringle and Fiddes (Th: 1970), Mitchell and Dawson (As: 1973), McAnarney *et al.* (Ar: 1974), and Swift *et al.* (D: 1967) used non-disabled children as controls, the variation in the criterion used (maladjustment, behavioural disturbance, emotional difficulty, poor adjustment, etc.) makes it difficult to compare their results.

Gayton and Friedman (1973) in the USA review the literature on the effects of *cystic fibrosis* and report that several studies reflect the existence of some degree of emotional disturbance, but that accurate figures cannot be derived. They point out that many studies have used projective tests which they consider to be of dubious value, and they argue that the use of psychiatric interview requires independent validation if reasonable accuracy is to ensue.

The two major studies of cystic fibrosis in Britain are those of Burton (1975) and Cull (1974). While these studies do not always reach the high standards of objectivity suggested by Gayton and Friedman (*op.cit.*), they do use objective scales such as the Bristol Social Adjustment Guide (BSAG) (Stott, 1958, 1974) and the Taylor Manifest Anxiety Scale (TMAS) (1953). Using the former scale with 30 school-age children and controls, Burton found that children with cystic fibrosis were significantly (p < 0.05) more unforthcoming and under-reactive compared with the scale norms. She suggests that this is true for all children with chronic illness and that these reactions serve as a means of avoiding situations which might prove stressful.

Cull (*op.cit.*) also found that the children tended to under-react according to the BSAG scale, but she reports a mean anxiety level on the TMAS similar to the provided norms. Cull concluded that the literature on cystic fibrosis tends to overstate the extent of the children's problems. She found that the children tended to be realistically anxious, somewhat isolated from their peers (possibly as a result of their young appearance) and that older children tended to have spells of extreme anxiety about their appearance.

The evidence for the incidence of social and emotional problems in children with *spina bifida* have been summarized by Pilling (1973b) and Anderson and Spain (1977). The work of Kolin *et al.* (1971), Laurence and Tew (1971), Tew (1973), Fulthorpe (1974) and Tew and Laurence (1975) also contain useful findings, but samples are often small. Anderson and Spain's (1977) summary suggests that certain behavioural problems may be common among children with spina bifida, these being distractibility, passivity and lack of drive, and fearfulness and anxiety when coping with difficulties.

Emotional and behavioural disorders in children with certain chronic disorders (asthma, congenital heart disease, hæmophilia, diabetes) seem to be only slightly more frequent than in the general population (Linde *et al.*, 1966, 1970; Landtman *et al.*, 1968; Salk *et al.*, 1972; Pilling, 1973c). Further, where an operation has been successful in curing congenital heart disease, children's behavioural symptoms improve considerably (Landtman *et al.*, 1968; Linde *et al.*, 1970). Good adaptation on the part of children with diabetes is linked with both good control over the condition and parents' adaptation and attitude (Swift *et al.*, 1967; Watson, 1972).

In her thorough review of the problems of children with asthma Pilling (1975) concludes that 'the evidence suggests that there is a slightly higher rate of emotional disorder in asthmatical children than in children with other physical handicaps which cannot be regarded as psychosomatic. . . .' (*op.cit.*, p. 14). There may be some link between the severity of the asthma and the presence of psychiatric disorder (Rutter *et al.*, 1970b; Williams, 1975; Pilling, 1975). However, Pilling (*ibid.*) emphasizes the general lack of connection between physical and psychiatric disorders, in that, with most conditions not involving brain disorder there appeared to be no link between severity and psychiatric symptoms.

Adolescents

In the report of Younghusband *et al.* (1970) it was observed that at that time there was a paucity of research into the problems of the adolescent with disablement. The position has since improved somewhat, though not to the extent that Anderson and Spain (1977) felt unable to repeat the observation about paucity of research made in Younghusband *et al.*'s report.

The need for such research is emphasized by Shakespeare (1975) who suggests that adolescence may raise special problems for the child with disablement so that at that stage emotional problems are particularly likely to occur. Shakespeare also implies that an analysis of the experience of disablement into the distinct aspects described as impairment, disability and handicap is not without value in exploring the social and emotional problems characteristic of the adolescent experience of children with disablement. Thus she points out that the adolescent with loss of mobility is often unable to take part in many normal social activities particularly associated with this phase in life: dancing, athletics or even work. Hence many handicaps resulting from disabilities occur for the first time at adolescence. Shakespeare also points out that physical appearance becomes especially important in adolescence so that those impairments affecting appearance will handicap adolescents unduly.

Further, as Morgan (1972) has observed, adolescents with disablement may well find that their 'normal' peers do not expect them to engage in 'normal' adolescent behaviour such as swearing, smoking and sexual experimentation. So they are faced with a 'double-bind': they may wish to appear normal, but they are, in fact, expected to be somehow 'better' than normal. At the same time, they face situations in which it is difficult for them to act 'normally'.

While it is clear that adolescents with certain impairments and disabilities are liable to face handicaps of the kinds described above, it is less clear whether one can argue that coping with them results in a higher rate of 'emotional disturbance'. Relevant work has, however, been undertaken by Dorner (1975) who interviewed 46 adolescents (13 to 19 years, mean 16.4) with spina bifida to assess the extent to which they experienced emotional problems. His results indicated that most (39) of them sometimes felt tearful or wanted 'to get away from it all'. He compares these observations with the findings of Rutter *et al.* (1976) who reported that nearly half of a group of 14½-year-olds without impairments and disabilities experienced these symptoms. Dorner also found that the group, or at least the girls in it, had suicidal ideas at a higher rate than the 'normal' adolescents of Rutter *et al.*'s (*ibid.*) and Bagley's (1975) samples.

Other aspects of Dorner's study suggests that adolescents with disablement may have more depressive feelings than adolescents without disablement. However, comments by Rutter *et al.* on the pecularities of their sample (all located in the Isle of Wight and all aged 14½ years) suggests that conclusions based on a comparison between Dorner's and Rutter *et al.*'s results should be drawn with considerable caution and that, at the least, different influential intervening variables may be acting in the two studies.

Other studies supply useful information, but their generalizability is very doubtful. Hence, there is still a clear need of more carefully controlled generalized studies of adolescence and disablement. Thus, Lorber and Schloss (1973) studied only 58 adolescents and young adults (age range 14 to 22) with spina bifida without controls and Freeman (1970) has discussed the psychiatric problems of adolescents with cerebral palsy only. The ongoing study of Anderson and Clarke (1978) which attempts to assess the social and psychological adjustment of both adolescents with spina bifida and adolescents with cerebral palsy also has limitations in that controls are planned only for that phase of the research which discusses the experience of children with disablement who are in schools. In view of the problems which Rutter *et al.* (1976) suggest may arise for adolescents at work, in studies of this kind a control group at the post-school stage would seem to be highly desirable.

Finally, there is also some lack of research in Britain on the sexual experience of adolescents with disablement, the main and almost only work being that of Dorner (1977). By studying a group of adolescents (n = 63, age 13 to 19, mean 16.4) with spina bifida, he attempted to find out how adequate their knowledge and experience of sexual matters was. He found that parents and the school had been the major sources of information. Only 15 per cent learnt about sex from their peers, a considerably lower proportion than was found in Schofield's (1968) study of 'normal' teenagers. Some (45 per cent) knew how children were conceived; only seven were 'dating' at the time of interview, though 11 had done so in the past and almost all were interested in the idea. Sexual intercourse had been experienced by one subject – a girl. Worries and uncertainties were very common among the older adolescents.

Stigma

There is a general consensus among researchers that visible impairments and disabilities evoke negative attitudes in those without them and that these exert a considerable influence on the interactions which take place between the two groups. As Bloom (1976) writes, 'the real trouble lies not so much with the disability but in the extraordinary stigma that is such an inherent part of our culture' (*op.cit.*, p. 22).

Brimblecombe (1977) has described the effect of disablement on both sides of the divide. He suggests that, to those without impairments and disabilities, those with them appear strange or 'other'; that ignorance leads to fearfulness and to a failure of communication and that between disabled and non-disabled interaction is hard to establish. Those with impairments and disabilities feel powerless and subject to the solutions which the rest of society deem appropriate.

The stigma to which children with disablement are subjected by their peers has also been closely studied by Richardson and his associates (Richardson *et al.*, 1961; Richardson and Royce, 1968; Richardson and Emerson, 1970; Richardson, 1971, 1976). Psychometric methods were used which involved presenting groups of pictures to schoolchildren who were then asked to rank them in order of preference. Richardson *et al.* suggest that their results imply a high degree of cultural uniformity in attitudes to children with disablement among the children studied. An important difference between the girls and the boys studied was that girls felt that impairment of appearance including obesity was worse than functional impairment, while boys took the opposite view. The observation of Richardson and Royce (1968) that the colour of the children in the pictures does not affect the rank-ordering led them to the view that impairments and disabilities influence children's performances more than race. However, Katz *et al.* (1976) have shown that, in practice, the reverse is often the case.

In Israel, Chigier and Chigier (1968) have reported similar findings to those of Richardson and his colleagues with the same series of pictures, though the ranking of the pictures was also influenced by the cultural stereotype and by the degree to which the child is successfully socialized into the cultural set of norms.

Richardson (1976) draws on his own research and that of Kleck *et al.* (1966, 1968) to summarize research findings on the behaviour of those without disablement, including children, towards their peers with it. He also points out the implications of the research findings for persons, children or adults, with disablement. He suggests that further research merely establishing the existence of stigma is superfluous. Rather, what is required is research investigating how stigma operates in complex social situations. People are generally unaware of the subtle changes in interaction which they instigate in the presence of individuals from minority groups.

The next section of this chapter, on the isolation of the child with disablement, may clarify some of the issues relating to stigma, though other factors than stigma – lack of mobility, parental attitudes, etc. – are obviously involved.

Social isolation

Two elements of isolation are particularly relevant to children with disablement. These are isolation in social contacts and isolation at school. Research into the factors influencing friendship choices is particularly relevant to these themes and this also is reviewed below.

On the amount of social contact experienced by children with disablement compared with controls, Butler *et al.*'s (1976) data supply useful detailed findings. In general, it was found that children with disablement had about a third less contact with local friends than control children but had similar rates of contact to the controls with friends from other districts.

There was variation between children with different disorders: children with muscular dystrophy and spina bifida had more contact with friends than those with cerebral palsy. It was also found, not surprisingly, that those with more serious disablement were generally more limited in their social contacts. Jarvis (1978) corroborates this last observation with the finding that fewer than 50 per cent of children in self-propelled wheelchairs had any local friends at all.

Compared with Butler *et al.*'s detailed and comprehensive study, earlier work (Watson, D: 1972; Cull, CF: 1974; Burton, CF: 1975; Mitchell and Dawson, As: 1973) does little more than confirm that the social experience and activities of children with disablement are more restricted than those of their peers without it. However, Dorner's (SB: 1975) observation that relationships of adolescents with disablement out of school were related to the type (special or ordinary) of school attended carries with it the possibility of adding a new dimension to the work on the issue. Dorner suggested that isolation was much more likely to occur when the young person had attended a special school. However, his sample is small and he does not make clear the extent to which social relationships occur with peers without disablement and the degree to which these take place between the same or opposite sex. He does, however, confirm Anderson's (1973) findings that girls seem more able to overcome the problems that lead to isolation than boys.

Anderson's study (*op.cit.*) used sociometric techniques to compare the relationships of 73 junior schoolchildren with those of controls. The children were asked to write down the names of those with whom they would most like to play, those with whom they best liked to sit and those with whom they would like to go if they were moved to another class. Children with congenital abnormalities were ranked relatively highly; those with spina bifida and cerebral palsy had the lowest rankings. The major functional limitations and inconvenience appeared to have little effect on sociometric status. Anderson (*op.cit.*) reports many more informative findings, some of which have since been confirmed by Cope and Anderson (1977) in a similar, though more restricted, study of children in special units of ordinary schools. Evaluation of the findings is, however, complicated by the transport problems experienced by the children with disablement; all but three of the children in special units lived some distance from their school.

Further evidence on the social relationships of children with disablement is provided by a study of these children with disablement in pre-school education by Clark *et al.* (1977). This work was undertaken for the Warnock Committee on Special Education (1978) and included an observational study of children with disablement and controls in both a nursery school and a playgroup. The time spent by the children on various activities was recorded. The significant differences between the children with disablement and the controls are listed by Clark *et al.* (*op.cit.*, p. 62). These are that the children with disablement are:

    i.   more likely to play alone,
    ii.   less likely to play with others,
    iii.   slightly more likely to be alone with an adult,
    iv.   likely to spend a similar time in a group with an adult and children,
    v.   less likely to engage in imaginative play,
    vi.   more likely to engage in non-specific activity, in listening to others or watching other activities,
    vii.   equally likely to communicate with adults and children for a similar amount of time,
    viii.   more likely to communicate less with other children,
    ix.   more likely to have one rather than two-way speech patterns.

It is difficult to see how these findings should be interpreted without further studies in which specific hypotheses about behaviour and interaction are tested. Thus it may be that the restricted functioning of most children with disablement can result in delayed learning of some kinds of activity. Alternatively, it may reduce the extent to which they can participate in them. Equally, however, peers may be unwilling to involve children with disabilities in their play because of their 'differentness'. As a result children with disablement are forced to participate less and observe more so that they have restricted opportunities of developing their playing skills.

In both surveys of cystic fibrosis (Cull, 1974; Burton, 1975) problems relating to schooling are mentioned. They suggest that after entry to school the children demonstrate anxiety about their physique, display self-consciousness and show alarm about illness. They found that the children were generally less sociable and more isolated than their peers. Cull's cœliac controls did not show these characteristics.

Teasing from peers has been reported in several studies (Dorner, SB: 1977; Anderson, 1973). The teasing could amount to bullying among boys. In general, however, teasing was not a serious problem and often amounted to no more than curiosity (Cope and Anderson, 1977; Halliwell and Spain, 1977).

Four important components in social isolation often lacked by children with diabilities are referred to by Anderson (1973) following Gold (1958). These are:

i.   social and emotional characteristics centring round the concepts of 'friendliness' and 'fun to be with';
ii.   expertise – knowing how to do things generally;
iii. 'associational' characteristics as shown by indices of similarity;
iv.   coercive resources – strength, prowess, etc.

Similarly, Canter and Barnitt (1978) suggest three major components to friendship: similarity, compatibility and reciprocity. Children with disablement may well be hampered by their obvious dissimilarity and their lack of resources for reciprocity. However, though the researches mentioned above, as that by Cope and Anderson (1977), raise important issues and provide fertile ground for hypotheses about the mechanisms of and the reasons for the relative social isolation of children with disablement in school and out, definitive work on that subject still remains to be undertaken. At the least, it is clear that other factors than the mere presence of physical disablement may be involved in social isolation. Educational problems and, indeed, teachers' and parents' attitudes may serve to influence the extent to which the child with disablement may well contribute to this perception and increase his or her isolation. If this is the case, the self-concept or self-image of the child may be an important factor in the experience of isolation and stigma.

Self-image

The issue of the self-image of children with disablement has received a fair amount of discussion from American researchers and is summarized by Safilios-Rothschild (1970). Mattson's (1972) and Feinberg *et al.*'s (1977) work is fairly typical of recent work. They suggest respectively that illness (hæmophilia) and operations may result in changes or distortions in body image.

Clifford (1969) studied the self-concepts of a group of children with asthma and compared them with a group of children with cleft palates, but found no major differences between them. However, Goldberg (1974) compared children with congenital heart disease with children with facial burns and found differences between them which led him to suggest that the self-image of the child with disablement was most affected by visible impairment even if serious disability did not ensue.

The whole subject of self-image is blurred by the variability in the concept as used by different researchers (Schurr *et al.*, 1970). Further, some versions of the concept seem likely to vary within an individual from day to day. Gouldner (1971) distinguishes between 'self-esteem', deriving from consensual validation from others, and 'self-regard', deriving from conflictual validation and the individual's sense of his 'potency' and autonomy (*op.cit.*, pp. 220–1). The last mentioned concepts are useful because it can be hypothesized that parents who seldom stigmatize their child maintain for him a vital area in which self-esteem can be won. If, however, they over-protect him, he cannot gain access to new situations and exceed their expectations in these. Hence his capability of developing self-potency is curtailed.

It may also be that Richardson *et al.*'s (1964) finding that children with disablement were aware of and shared peer values, but that they were also unable to live up to some of the expectations of the value-system, can be interpreted along these lines. These children manage, just as all people with or without disablement do, to find ways of gaining self-esteem and self-regard from activities which are in no sense close to the ideal. In other words, they gain a self-concept which matches their capabilities, just as most employed persons gain self-potency from the job they do, even though all jobs are not equally valued in society.

Employment and, possibly, marriage, may, in fact, pose the most severe problems to young people with disablement since they are the most widely sought signs of social status. Hence in young adulthood the person with disablement may have to face the most severe challenge to his or her self-esteem and self-regard. At this stage, their earlier sources of support, home and school, are no longer legitimated.

Adjustment to disablement

Pless and Pinkerton (1975) review research on the influence of chronic illness in childhood on the child's personality. Their findings may be summarized as follows:

1.   Among children with chronic disorder, most of those studied have a greater degree of frequency of maladjustment than do their healthy peers of comparable background.

2.   Certain features of the disease – age of onset, manner of progression, prognosis, the characteristic type of the resulting disability, especially its severity and duration – each affect the adjustment of the child.

3.   Some characteristics of the child prior to the illness, especially his intelligence, personality, coping style and any other assets he may possess – attractiveness, charm, special skills, etc. – influence his ability to cope with any future chronic illness.

4.   Coping is also influenced by the strength and resilience of family relationships and the extent to which the family is burdened by external pressures and stresses.

5.   Within the family, the attitudes of the parents, especially the mother, are of crucial importance. The feelings the parents have about the illness, the effect it has on their lives and those of the

other children in the family, the direct day-to-day burdens disability imposes, all have a direct bearing on the child's coping capacity.

Not all these findings can be accepted without qualification. Thus, it has been suggested in an earlier section of this chapter that, when there is no neurological disorder, a disabled child is only slightly more prone to maladjustment than a non-disabled child. It would then follow that neurological impairment is usually the main factor in maladjustment.

Good adaptation is another concept that needs delimitation (Miller, 1970). Mattson (1972), whose work was briefly discussed at the beginning of this chapter, suggests that good adaptation takes place when the child accepts realistic limitations and has little need for secondary gains from his disablement. He further suggests that well-adapted children are able to find satisfaction in compensatory physical and intellectual activities and in successfully mastering exacerbations of their condition. However, Tinkelman *et al.* (1976) refer to the tendency to shift emphasis towards the positive aspects of disablement as a means of ameliorating the guilt and anxiety caused by envy of others. Hence, what Mattson sees as good adaptation is seen by Tinkelman and his colleagues as the opposite.

Myers *et al.* (1970) and Pless and Pinkerton (1975) on the whole agree with Mattson. They see the use of mechanisms for coping, including withdrawal and denial, as 'good' adjustment. They point out that 'acceptance' is not the same as adaptation, since the unworried optimism that children often entertain about the prognosis of their condition does not appear to hinder their development (Minde *et al.*, 1972; Herskowitz and Marks, 1977); rather the opposite (Cull, 1974).

Many factors have been suggested as influencing adaptation. Anderson and Spain (1977) and Pilling in her several reviews (1972; 1973a, b, c; 1975) regard parental adaptation as the key. Davis (1975) and Fox (1977) see the child's attitude to himself and his disablement, as mediated by the parents or caretaker, as a crucial factor in adaptation. However, there is a lack of data to estimate the influence of many other suggested factors in adaptation, such as the coping mechanisms employed. Lynch and Arndt (1973) suggest that young children tend to cope by denying frustration, while older children tend to cope by blaming themselves, but corroborative studies are required.

CHAPTER SIX
The Siblings of Children with Physical Disablement

Quality of the evidence

Most of the data on the problems of siblings of a child with disablement have been obtained by parental report rather than by direct questioning and observation. Hence, though researchers generally conclude that the kinds of experience discussed in this chapter put these siblings under considerable strain, the evidence is sometimes circumstantial.

A related problem with the data available on this subject is that some researchers appear to have relied for their information mainly on their own empathy to understand the emotional problems of the siblings. For example, Kew (1975) writes:

> The still surface of the pool of our experience is broken by an ill wind: we feel disturbed . . . .
> This is hardly the language of science, but it is precisely here that the mistake has crept in, for we are not dealing with the language of science but with the subjective language of experience . . . .
> When we say that a child is disturbed we are not classifying a definitive condition from which he is suffering, we are merely reaching out to his experience of himself and of the world in which he lives (*op.cit.*, p. 29).

While the poetry of such a statement is doubtless appealing, it diverts attention from difficult methodological problems.

One such problem is related to the tendency for parents, professionals and even researchers to perceive a child in terms of the label attached to him and to adjust their expectations accordingly. It is all too easy therefore to suggest that the siblings in question will be likely to have problems and to interpret their behaviour accordingly (which, in effect, applies a courtesy stigma to them). A researcher who adjusts his expectations in this way is liable to set up a framework in his research which makes him prone to understand the siblings' behaviour in terms which reflect the current cultural value-system and stereotypes and which, therefore, confirm the prejudices inherent in that system. To give a simple example: the boy who is seen to be hitting his disabled brother would be liable to be regarded as emotionally disturbed by a researcher who normally accepts a cultural value along the lines of 'you don't hit cripples'. Yet, if the sibling does not hit his brother he is also liable to be seen as 'repressing his aggression' even though he may have reached the stage where cultural values are internalized.

Hence the researcher who attempts 'reaching out' to the sibling's 'experience of himself and of the world in which he lives' is in danger of taking as his starting point the assumption that those experiences are bound to be culturally abnormal. He is asking how the sibling adapts to this abnormal situation, yet, for the sibling, the family he lives in is his *normal* situation. Perhaps it is not unfair to state fairly categorically that as the empathizing observer and the child in his situation are really most unlikely to share the same value system as regards disablement, empathy is an unprofitable method of acquiring research evidence.

The orthodox way of overcoming this problem is to establish a definition of disturbance which, while it may ignore the meanings and feelings of the sibling to some degree, will at least attempt to relate the concept of disturbance to a range of behaviours which are recognized as indicators of it. In doing this, data are obtained which can be compared to those obtained from 'normal' children. Some research is reported below, especially in the section on the incidence in siblings of emotional and behavioural problems, in which this approach is adopted.

Family problems and parental neglect

The methodological problem referred to in the previous section is particularly exemplified in much of the literature on the lack of parental attention devoted to siblings of children with disablement.

Obviously, parents may have to ration the time and attention they give to non-disabled siblings, but there is a tendency in the literature to regard this as automatically indicative of over-protection of the child with disablement and of potential problems for the siblings.

Many writers (Schaffer, 1964; Landtman *et al.*, 1968; Berggreen, 1971; Bentovim, 1972; Salk *et al.*, 1972) suggest that non-disabled siblings are neglected by their parents because of the parents' pre-occupation with the child with disablement. Indeed, Berggreen (*op.cit.*) goes so far as to describe the neglect as 'frequently very gross'.

The literature on family therapy (e.g. Minuchin, 1974; Waldron-Skinner, 1976) tends to place emphasis on the way that problems in families may be ventilated through a 'scapegoat' non-disabled child. Thus, Poznanski (1969) suggests that '. . . parents may hold back some or all their negative feelings from the handicapped child and consistently "take it out" on the healthy siblings' (*op.cit.*, 1969, p. 233). She also suggests that siblings may develop problems as a result of emotional neglect.

Researchers also comment on the effect of a child with disablement on the family as a whole, though their findings are diverse. Thus Schaffer (1964) considers that there is a danger of 'over-cohesiveness' in the family. On the other hand Jaehnig (1974), while he considers that sharing the task of caring for the child serves to draw the family together, also regards this as promoting healthy adjustment by the siblings. Similarly, Lloyd-Bostock (1976) reports that parents felt that the effect on siblings of having a child with disablement in the family was wholly positive. Perhaps it can be suggested that when parents attempt to construct their non-disabled children's experience of dealing with their sibling as positive, this may well be the definition which is accepted by the child.

As is remarked at the beginning of this chapter, much of the survey evidence on the lack of parental attention given to siblings of children with disablement depends on the recorded views of the parents themselves. Thus Cull (CF: 1974) reports that 59 per cent of mothers said that they felt that their non-impaired children were disadvantaged or deprived in various ways. In Burton's sample (CF: 1974) 39 per cent of mothers and 26 per cent of fathers felt this to be the case. The incidence of reported deprivation in both these studies appeared to be unrelated to family size or the severity of the condition. In addition, it is suggested that parents may feel more attached to the child with disablement than to the siblings. Burton (*ibid.*, p. 188 and p. 233) does not quantify the extent to which this occurs, but Cull (*op.cit.*) found that about a third of the parents studied said that they obtained more pleasure from the child with disablement than from the other siblings.

Relations between siblings and the child with disablement

Many writers suggest that the relations between a child with disablement and his siblings are often strained. Kew (1975) discusses 'characteristic' reactions which include rivalry, jealousy, disguised jealousy, displaced aggression, fear and anxiety. Hostility is discussed by Podeanu-Czehofsky (1975) who argues that siblings are sometimes cruel towards the child. Schutt (1977) also refers to jealousy and resentment as common reactions and adds that siblings may suffer from feelings of embarrassment because their brother or sister has a visible impairment. Jealousy is also referred to by Burton (CF: 1975) who found it in 22 per cent of older and 27 per cent of younger children. Hewett's (CP: 1970) and Woodburn's (1973) samples of parents put the prevalence of jealousy in siblings at about 30 per cent.

Woodburn (1973) also refers to resentment, reporting that half the children of the two-thirds of the parents in the sample who said they spent more time on the child with disablement were said to resent this. On the other hand, Richards and McIntosh (1973) reported resentment in only seven of the 86 families studied, while Hewett (1970) found that the incidence of sibling rivalry was no higher in families containing a child with disablement than among the general population.

Butler *et al.*'s research (1978) provides survey evidence on several relevant matters. They report that 20 per cent of siblings of children with disablement had problems with homework, 44 per cent with looking after possessions, and 34 per cent in entertaining friends or playing with them. In addition, 39 per cent were reported as being jealous of the child with disablement while 37 per cent had problems other than those mentioned above.

Butler *et al.* also provide even more detailed findings. With homework the major problems were interruptions, noise, emotional upset and destruction of books or papers. With possessions, most problems arose from interference and destructiveness. Interference was also the main problem when friends were entertained. In general, siblings with a mental impairment caused most problems.

Behavioural and social problems

As was mentioned in the first section of this chapter, most of the research into the emotional and behavioural problems of the siblings of children with disablement does not allow one to make a comparison with children without such a sibling. However, some researchers (e.g. Cull, 1974; Tew and Laurence, 1973) have used the Bristol Social Adjustment Guide (BSAG: Stott, 1974) with samples and controls to obtain data.

Cull (CF: 1974) found that 42 per cent of a sample of 72 siblings of children with disablement showed signs of 'under-reaction' as compared with 19 per cent of controls, while 42 per cent as compared with 22 per cent of controls over-reacted. Over-reaction is generally regarded as more serious as it is related to delinquency in some children (Stott, 1974). Cull also records that 31 per cent of siblings of children with cystic fibrosis were reported by their parents as having behavioural problems as compared to 15 per cent of siblings of children with cœliac disease. Burton (CF: 1975) does not offer comparable data, but does note that 37 per cent of mothers and 28 per cent of fathers reported having problems with the impaired child's siblings. The problems, included rebelliousness, resentment and bed-wetting. Tew and Laurence (1973) used the BSAG with a small sample of siblings of children with spina bifida and a control group. They report that there was four times the risk of maladjustment for the experimental group than the control.

Other researchers, (e.g. McMichael, 1971; MacKeith, 1973; Kew, 1975) report relevant findings, though the work on which these are based often lacks controls or is based on small samples. Gath's (1973) research on the siblings of children with Down's syndrome, however, used controls and the sample is of reasonable size (174 siblings). Gath reports that 20 per cent of the siblings and ten per cent of the controls were rated as 'deviant' on either of Rutter's A and B scales (Rutter *et al.*, 1970b). Similarly, 'anti-social' children were found to be more common among the siblings than the controls. There were no statistically significant differences in behaviour according to whether the sibling was born before or after the child with disablement, except that all those rated deviant who were born afterwards showed behaviour which could be described in this way. Further, the findings showed that for the boys there was no higher prevalence of behavioural disorders in the sample compared with the controls. In fact, all the differences between the sample and the controls stemmed from the increased incidence of disorders among the female siblings. In a later paper, Gath (DS: 1974) reports that the most vulnerable siblings were girls who were either first-born in the family or were three or more years older than the sibling with disablement; younger girl siblings were seldom affected.

A tendency to anti-social behaviour in siblings was also found when the mother suffered from a chronic neurosis or where the family were working class. Gath suggests that those siblings who were most affected were those exposed to most domestic responsibility and who were regarded as failing in the educational system. The following quotation summarizes Gath's findings:

> The indications are that the sibling, whose parents and teachers rate as deviant, more often comes from a family where the mongol child is only one of many problems, particularly those of having a father in a poorly paid occupation, as well as the sheer size of the family. The elder sisters of mongol children in this study can be described as receiving more than their fair share of community care, and the ill-effects of this stress will be felt by them and by the community well into the future (Gath, 1974).

It should be emphasized that these observations relate only to the siblings of children with Down's syndrome. The studies of children with cystic fibrosis and their siblings undertaken by Cull (1974) and Burton (1975) as well as Tew and Laurence's (1973) work among siblings of children with spina bifida do not report such clear-cut findings. However, Gath's and other work (Grossman, 1974; Wilkin, 1978) does suggest that it would be useful to investigate further the relationship between behaviour disturbance in siblings of children with disablement and the extent of their participation in the care of the child.

The kind of social problem likely to be observed among siblings of children with disablement is indicated by Kew (1975, p. 122) and by Anderson and Spain (1977). The latter suggest that:

> . . . siblings are going to have to come to terms with the attitudes to their handicapped brother or sister of other people, including their peers from outside the home. They are often quick to perceive the social stigma attached to handicap and this may be reflected in their unwillingness to bring their friends into their home (*op.cit.*, p. 81).

Available survey evidence, however, suggests that social difficulties only arise for a minority of those children. Thus the Isle of Wight study (Rutter *et al.*, 1970b, p. 335) suggests that there are difficulties for only five per cent of children with a sibling with physical disablement. However, Butler *et al.* (1978) found that 34 per cent of siblings of all children with disablement in their sample had some problems in inviting their friends home.

Butler *et al.* also found that 52 per cent of mothers did not feel that their children were called upon to make special explanation of their disabled sibling to friends, while 35 per cent felt that while an explanation was necessary it did not present a problem. Only 18 per cent believed that their non-impaired children had problems in explaining their sibling's condition or were unduly reticent about him.

Gath (DS: 1973) also reports relevant information. She found that the most common problems of siblings of children with Down's syndrome reported by parent and teachers were unpopularity or difficulty in peer relations. Further than this, and apart from the citation of incidents where the sibling has become involved in fights with other children over name-calling (Woodburn, 1973, p. 250; Hill, 1976), there is on the whole little evidence on the social difficulties of siblings of children with disablement. Perhaps it is reasonable to suggest that the sibling is in a more favourable position to avoid accepting a courtesy stigma than are his parents. Nevertheless, as there has been little theoretical or empirical work on how this is managed by children of different ages, further observational and sociometric studies are clearly required.

Conclusion

On the 'facts' of the problems of siblings of children with disablement, Butler *et al.*'s (1978) evidence is most comprehensive, though it is of somewhat doubtful validity, being based on parental report. About a third of children were felt by parents to consider their family 'different' from those of others, mainly because of restrictions or disruption. On siblings' general attitude towards the child with disablement, Butler *et al.* report that 40 per cent of mothers thought that the siblings felt the same as they would to any brother or sister, 33 per cent said that they were especially loving and protective, 19 per cent said that the siblings' feelings were mixed or inconsistent, while only eight per cent were resentful or embarrassed.

Particularly helpful advice has been provided by Parfitt (1975). She argues that facts need to be explained to siblings so that they can understand the nature and the cause of their sibling's disablement and answer the questions of other children. She also recommends that children should be taught how to help their sibling and should be actively involved in planning his or her further care. Another recommendation by Jobling is for intuitive and physically reassuring support for siblings when young, and for verbal reassurance and the chance to help when older. The discussion of the possibility of feelings of jealousy and guilt and of 'skeleton in the cupboard' attitudes is also suggested.

CHAPTER SEVEN

Services provided for Families with a Child with Disablement

Introduction

The first part of this chapter examines the literature concerning research on services provided by three identifiable professional groups – doctors, social workers and health visitors. In the last two sections the literature relating to care services and to a few 'miscellaneous' services is reviewed. We make no profound apologies for the fragmentary nature of this last section of the chapter; much of the work described is novel, either in content, approach or both, so that it was difficult to be sure which of the papers and projects would be deemed significant in the future.

Generally speaking, the research on the subject of this chapter as a whole is of two kinds. First, there are fact-finding surveys in which the amount of contact with or help received from professionals such as doctors and social workers is recorded. Secondly, there is a good deal of research which inquires rather more closely into the nature of the contact between the professional who provides or mediates the service and the parents who receive it. This latter research is often concerned to inquire into the effect of the trend of recent decades to professionalize contacts between the providers and receivers of services. In this chapter, research of the first kind is concentrated on, though comments will be made on research of the second kind in part of the final chapter.

The general practitioner

Many researchers have pointed out that, as a general rule, parents of children with disablement rely on hospital doctors rather than GPs when problems arise (Fox, 1971; Burton, 1975; Harrison, 1977). This is not surprising since the average GP is likely to have only three such children in his practice at any one time (Goddard and Rubissow, 1977). At the same time, there are many instances reported in which the GP is felt by parents to be useful. Thus Hewett (1970) mentions cases in which the GP had either provided regular support or had helped to make contact with other services. It seems that even when GPs lack expertise, they are often seen as supportive by appearing to parents as an ally rather than an opponent. This could be a factor operating behind Butler *et al.*'s finding that the GP was the most frequently mentioned (31 per cent) source of advice (1978, p. 91).

Relationships between parents and GPs sometimes suffer because parents feel that their GPs are sometimes slow in diagnosing new symptoms (Anderson and Spain, 1977, p. 71) or late-onset conditions such as diabetes (Watson, 1972).

Hospital doctors

As is mentioned above, hospital doctors and consultants are the main source of medical support for parents of children with disablement because of their greater experience with particular diseases and disorders (Fox, 1971; Burton, 1975; Harrison, 1977). From the evidence that exists on parents' experiences with hospitals it would appear that the technical proficiency of the personnel is high, though parents sometimes feel that they rank low in humanity (Fox, 1971).

A major complaint about hospital medical services is that parents often see a different doctor every visit. Thus Hewett (1970) found that mothers who saw the same doctor on each visit were more satisfied than those who saw a variety of doctors. She suggests that this is not simply the result of familiarity but arises from parents not having to use a large part of a short consultation merely for supplying background details.

For many disorders, once the child's condition has stabilized, visits to hospital seem to take place about once every six months (Hewett, 1970; Bradshaw, 1977). In Hewett's sample, parents rarely saw the doctor for more than ten minutes. When this is matched against Anderson and Spain's report (1977) that in Greater London out-patients' appointments usually involved one to two hours' travelling, and Woodburn's finding that the majority of journeys took 'from two to five hours from the time of leaving home to return' (p. 198), with 23 per cent spending more than five hours on travel, one can appreciate that a ten-minute consultation with a strange doctor unaware of the details of the case would be likely to cause resentment even if all that is medically necessary can be completed in the time.

Health visitors

Reports on the frequency of contact between mothers and health visitors vary considerably, perhaps because of local influences. Wilkin (1978) suggests a low level of contact generally, reporting that only 17 per cent of all mothers had seen a district nurse or health visitor in the year prior to interview. Contact appears to be much greater for mothers of children with disablement. Thus Baldwin (1976) reports that about a quarter of her sample had regular contact with a health visitor while about 60 per cent had occasional contact. Similarly, Hewett (*op.cit.*) found that 75 per cent of the children had been visited by a health visitor, 40 per cent being seen at least three times a year. Spain reports the regular visiting of 33 per cent and occasional visiting of a further 40 per cent. By contrast, Harrison (1977) reports little contact with health visitors for children with Perthes disease and cystic fibrosis.

Goddard and Rubissow's study of this matter (1977) is the only one which uses direct controls. In their sample, they found that children with disablement were visited, on average, 7.8 times per annum while controls were visited 4.7 times.

On whether the visiting is of value to mothers, reports vary. Walker *et al.* (1971), Voysey (1975) and Anderson and Spain (1977), found that mothers felt that health visitors lacked knowledge and expertise on specific conditions: 'In most cases, however, mothers simply found their health visitor 'nice' and quite enjoyed their visits . . . In general health visitors do not appear to give either direct or indirect help to parents of disabled children.' (Voysey, 1975, pp. 180–1). However, Burton (CF: 1975) suggests that the skills of the health visitors can be helpful towards obtaining diagnosis when impairment is of late onset, though the main element of contact appreciated by parents refers to moral support, listening and taking parents' misgivings seriously.

Fox (1971, 1975) found that health visitors were, in fact, the preferred source of support for about 35 per cent of his sample, being seen as 'maternal' figures. He also reports that their functions were not clear to most mothers: they thought of her as part of 'the welfare'. Similarly, Baldwin (1976) records that 60 per cent of mothers of children under five who were visited found the visits useful; their practical assistance and, more often, their being someone to talk to were seen as being of most help.

Social workers

Children with disablement and their families do not appear to receive much more support from social workers than do other families, though support might be increasing. Thus, Butler *et al.* (1976) found that only 23 per cent of such families had received help from social workers in the year preceding interview, while in their later survey (1978) they found that 51 per cent of families had a visit from a social worker in the preceding year. However, 56 per cent of these families expressed some dissatisfaction with the service they received. Common complaints about social workers were that their turnover was too high, that they were too young, inexperienced or overworked, and that they had insufficient knowledge about benefits. Other unfavourable comments referred to the social work service itself – its red tape and the length of the referral process. Some of the complaints, however, arise from the mismatch between what the service aims to provide and the main needs felt by parents of children with disablement. It seems that some parents want people who can supply their need of information efficiently, some want services from the local authority which require the mediation of a social worker, while others merely want some understanding person to talk to.

McMichael (1971) found that all families in her sample had contact with social workers. However, her data were gathered almost ten years earlier, before the present structure of social work services had been established. She found that visits were welcomed by 68 per cent of mothers, were tolerated by 16 per cent and were resented by only four per cent; the replies of the remaining 12 per cent were not analysed. Visits were frequent and regular, in contrast to reports from the later reorganized services. Thus Jaehnig (1974) reports that less than half his sample had annual contact and Moss and Silver (1972) found that 37 per cent of mothers had had no contact with welfare services in the preceding year. Similarly, Baldwin (1976) and Bradshaw (1977) report that most Family Fund applicants had contact with social services only for specific things. Baldwin (*op.cit.*) even suggests that her figures (shown in Table 3, below) may over-estimate the contact as parents may have associated all visitors together as 'the welfare', just as Fox (1971) found for health visitors.

Table 3: Family Fund mothers' contact with social services
(Baldwin, 1976, p. 11)

Frequency of contact		No.	%
Regularly (at least every four months)		33	10.9
4 months to one year		42	13.9
Occasionally, i.e. for specific things		183	60.4
Never		38	12.5
Don't know/remember		7	2.3
	Total	303	100.0

In the same study, however, 62 per cent of mothers found social workers helpful or at least sympathetic, the rest felt that they were unable to give practical advice, visited too infrequently, changed too often or were too young or inexperienced.

The amount of contact with social workers is related to the degree of disablement, the most severely impaired having most contact. Butler *et al.* (1978) report that 72 per cent of mothers with doubly incontinent children, 50 per cent with singly incontinent children and 44 per cent with continent children had contact in the year prior to interview. Similarly, 71 per cent of mothers with a child confined to a wheelchair had contact, compared with 50 per cent whose child was semi-ambulant and 45 per cent whose child was ambulant.

Other criteria may also be related to obtaining the services of social workers. In a study of parents of mentally retarded children, Wilkin (1978) found that contact and the provision of services were related to whether or not the child was waiting for admission to residential care. Eighty per cent of those awaiting admission and 57 per cent of those who were not had been visited by a social worker in the year prior to interview. Also 40 per cent of the former, but only seven per cent of the latter had received help from the local authority.

In a similar study undertaken by the Medway Community Council, Silver (1976) found that contact with social workers and the receipt of local authority services was less among older parents, although there was no decrease in the number of problems experienced. Indeed, some families with the maximum number of problems on the scale used by Silver had much less contact with both social workers and health visitors than had those with fewer problems.

A straightforward explanation of the amount of help received from social workers comes from Bradshaw and Lawton's (1978) report on stress in families. It seems that mothers who scored highly on Rutter's Malaise Scale (Rutter *et al.*, 1970b) were more likely to have contact with a social worker. To this extent, therefore, the evidence supports a view that those with most problems receive most help. However, it is clear from the research cited in this section that satisfaction with the social work services is not particularly high nor, as Butler *et al.* (1978) report, does it necessarily increase with more contact or service provision.

Care services

Short-term care

The aim of short-term care is, of course, to give temporary relief to parents burdened with a child with disabilities. Baldwin (1976) describes the ideal short-term care programme as providing:

> . . . a resource for parents to call on when they themselves are exhausted, when the child was particularly difficult to care for, when other members of the family were ill or siblings showed signs of needing more attention than it was possible for them to have while the mother's energies were concentrated on the handicapped child (*op.cit.*, p. 24).

As usual, the reality falls short of this ideal. Hewett (CP: 1970) suggests that short-term care, even when it is provided in a home-like family unit, may be equivalent to a stay in hospital for the child. Hewett considers that a balance has to be drawn between the disadvantages to the child and the needs of the parents, '. . . it is often essential that the mothers of handicapped children and possibly the rest of the family should be given some respite from caring for them. There is a genuine conflict of interest here' (*op.cit.*, p. 72). In Hewett's sample of mothers, 41 per cent had accepted short-term care at some stage while a further 14 per cent said they would accept it if it were offered. In a larger and more broadly-based sample, Family Fund researchers found it both less popular and less used (Baldwin, 1976). Seventy-six per cent of mothers had never had their child cared for away from home, about 13 per cent had made use of the facility once only, and 11 per cent had made use of it several times. When asked if they wanted short-term care to be provided or wanted it more often, about 74 per cent indicated that they did not.

Baldwin (1976) suggests that parents' expectations are influenced by their preconceptions about the care actually provided. Limited experience will reduce demand, but the high proportion of care provided in the apparently inappropriate long-term subnormality hospitals also reduces it. Probably parents are reluctant to commit their children to an environment which they feel to be unlikely to match standards of care they themselves provide.

As with other services there appears to be some danger that short-term care will become a 'crisis' facility. In a study of the parents of children with intellectual impairments, Wilkin (1978) found that parents of children awaiting residential care were more likely to be provided with short-term care.

The work of certain units, notably Honeylands and Baildon House, providing short-term care has been described by Pugh and Russell (1977). The work of Honeylands, also mentioned by Brimblecombe (1974) and Goddard and Rubissow (1976), is currently being studied in research financed by the DHSS. Baildon House uses foster parents as the basis for its relief care. Somerset Social Service Department also make use of foster parents in this way (Garrett, 1978).

Long-term care

Long-term residential care for children with physical disablement has received little research attention, though Oswin's work (1971) has provided useful information on the varieties of experience which children face in long-term care. Her later work (1977, 1978) on the same theme concentrates on children with multiple impairments in mental hospitals. Almost all work on long-term care refers to children with mental impairments. We refer to this work in the next paragraph.

Tizard and Grad (1961) found that admission was related to severity of impairment, particularly mental impairment. Jaehnig (1974) drew the same conclusion from his work, but argued that adverse social factors such as low income, poor housing and parental ill-health are also important determinants of admission. Baylay (1973) also isolated social factors and showed that poor maternal health and the absence of the husband from the home made institutional care more likely. It seemed that the young mildly-impaired children institutionalized sample came from homes where there were poor relationships and low standards of care. The older mildly-impaired children usually needed to be institutionalized simply because there was no one to look after them. When impairment was severe, the major factors favouring institutionalization were disabilities of behaviour, capacity and family functioning. Other researchers, such as Kellmer Pringle and Fiddes (Th: 1970), Shakespeare (1975) and Hewett (CP: 1976), also stress adverse family background together with poor prognosis and behaviour and sleep disturbance, as major determinants of institutionalization.

How far these findings relating to children with mental impairments also apply to children with physical impairments is unclear, though it seems that when the child has behavioural problems and poor home circumstances parents are more likely to ask for their child to have a place in a residential school (Pless, 1969). However, Hewett (1976) has suggested that as with short-term care most parents are unhappy about their child being in long-term residential care and that the decision that the child should receive such care or go to a residential school is usually made very reluctantly.

Financial provisions

(i) The Family Fund

As has been mentioned several times in this review, in recent years a good deal of financial help has become available to parents of children with disablement through the Family Fund. Reviewing the research on the Family Fund is a particularly daunting task for any outside researcher. Fortunately, the Director of the Family Fund Research Unit, now the Social Policy Research Unit at the University of York, has himself recently reviewed the work of the Fund (Bradshaw, 1980). We therefore refer here only to his earlier papers commenting on the take-up of the money made available by the Fund.

Bradshaw (1978a) has estimated that when the Fund was instituted in 1972 just over 100,000 families were eligible for help from the Fund on the basis of their children's disablement. In the first three years of the Fund about 29,000 families applied for help. In terms of their monthly rate, applications peaked in March 1974. Since that date and up to about the end of 1977 they have assumed a steady rate of about 550 per month. Bradshaw commented that the gradual levelling-off to this figure which took place:

> does not necessarily indicate that the Fund has now dealt with the demand and is merely receiving applications from newly disabled children. There is only a marginal tendency for more recent applicants to have younger children and the vast majority of applicants are still children who could have applied to the Family Fund from its onset (*op.cit.*, p. 159).

Bradshaw (*ibid.*) has also reported some interesting characteristics of those who applied to the Fund. In the first three years, applications tended to come from parents with children in middle childhood. Larger proportions of manual workers, single parents and parents with large families applied than statistical distributions would suggest as likely. There were also variations in take-up by region, much of which was explicable in terms of the social characteristics of the population.

In summarizing the work on take-up Bradshaw (*op.cit.*) draws the following conclusions:

1. The Family Fund is known to about half the famil — though only a third have applied.
2. The numbers applying could be increased by a hal again if fresh efforts were made to bring the Fur notice of families and provide more information to those who know about it.
3. Even with these efforts the total number of families who apply to the Fund is not likely to rise much beyond half of those who are eligible.
4. Any attempt to increase the number of applications to the Fund will inevitably result in more applications from families who are ineligible but it is probable that two out of every three will be eligible.
5. It is probable that those families who have applied to the Fund are on average in greater need than those who have not.
6. The main barrier to families claiming is ignorance – ignorance of the existence of the Fund, that it applies to them, or that they can get help with a particular item they need. There is no evidence that the stigma of demonstrating need might have prevented families from claiming. The strongest influence in determining the number of claims received by the Family Fund must be the low expectations of many of the families and their determination to soldier on without help. Bradshaw (1978a), pp. 173–4.

(ii) Statutory benefits

The two most important centrally-administered benefits for which children may be eligible are the Attendance Allowance and the Mobility Allowance. The former, as its name suggests, is allocated primarily on the basis of a person's attendance needs. It seems to be reaching the majority of those children who are eligible for it, though Bradshaw (1977) cites some evidence that about ten per cent of families with eligible children may not have applied. A potentially useful part of his work is a multivariate model which he has constructed. This enables those children whose applications for the Attendance Allowance appear to be misassessed to be identified so that a review can be asked for.

Baldwin (1975a) has also examined some of the problems that parents of children with disablement have found with the Attendance Allowance. She discusses the criticisms made of the benefit by parents and draws the conclusion that, whilst many of them cannot be justified they do serve to '. . . reflect the absence of a coherent policy for handicapped children and especially the absence of any element of compensation for disablement as such', (*op.cit.*, pp. 190–1).

The only evidence available in 1978 on the number of families eligible for and aware of the Mobility Allowance was conducted before the extension of the scheme to children (Butler *et al.*, 1978). The researchers concluded that there was adequate dissemination of information about the benefit. However, preliminary work by the University of York Social Policy Research Unit suggests that deciding eligibility may be particularly difficult when children are the claimants. Baldwin (1975b) has suggested that many disorders and impairments of children which are liable to cause mobility problems are not covered by the criteria for the benefit. She lists disorders thus:

> . . . uncontrolled epilepsy, conditions like cystic fibrosis which make children particularly susceptible to infections or adverse climatic conditions, children who are technically able to walk but only for a short distance, children who are at risk on public transport such as hæmophiliac children or those with very severe skin conditions, certain groups of blind and deaf children and children who are mentally subnormal . . . (*op.cit.*, p. 36).

The decision of the National Insurance Commissioner in adjudicating an appeal by the Secretary of State after a child with Down's syndrome had been awarded benefit (Decision CM.2/77) illustrates the kind of problems that can arise when the statutory provisions for the allowance have to be applied to cases of disablement which raise fundamental medical issues.

Other services

(i) Group work

Both in the USA and in Britain group work with parents of children with disablement has been recorded both in the research literature and in articles (Mattson and Agle, 1972; Lewis, 1972; Attwood, 1977; Loeb, 1977). Though no rigorous evaluation has been conducted, the benefits referred to include increase in self-esteem and less isolation (Mattson and Agle), improvement in parental attitude to the child and better knowledge of the disablement (Lewis).

(ii) Therapy

Some therapists, e.g. Glen Doman (1974), argue that by therapy the brain can be trained into new 'structures' hence improving function. More conventionally, emphasis is often placed on play and the provision of a broad range of experience to stimulate children with disablement (Newson, 1976; Levitt, 1975). Attempts have also been made to change mothers' style of interaction with their child. This particular kind of work is recorded in a series of papers by Tyler and Kogan (1972, 1977; Kogan *et al.*, 1974; Kogan and Tyler, 1973, 1976). They reported that mothers, in therapy with a child:

> . . . were often preoccupied with their ability to position the child's limbs properly at the expense of their awareness of his personal comfort or satisfaction, and that they frequently seemed to view the child's inability to perform as a demonstration of their own inadequacy in working with him. Mothers were so intent on achieving the desired goal that they repeatedly called the child's errors to his attention, and often failed to appreciate or support his less-than-successful efforts to comply (Kogan and Tyler, 1973).

The programme of instruction that was devised following this observation attempted to improve the style of interaction between mother and child. The mothers of 20 spastic children were given directions through an earphone and observed again three and nine months later. Improvements in interaction were significant nine months later in 16 cases, although other concomitant benefits such as a reduction in behavioural problems were not observed.

(iii) Home programmes

Dudzinski and Peters (1977) refer to a variety of home-based programmes in the USA (e.g. Pless and Satterwhite, 1972; Levitt and

Cohen, 1973; Fishman and Fishman, 1975). These were set up with the intention of avoiding the extremes of institutionalization and of unsupported home care for the children. Another example of a home programme is the 'home visitation' model, described by Shearer and Shearer (1972), in which a visiting professional teaches parents how to shape their child's behaviour and to develop his abilities and experiences. Other home programmes have worked in conjunction with parent groups or have made use of television. In their review, Dudzinski and Peters (1977) describe the factors which promote success in these programmes and warn that they may not be successful with all families.

British programmes on similar lines have tended to concentrate on the mentally impaired, but they generally provide support for the findings of the American work, such as that a prerequisite of success is that the parents rather than the visitor should see themselves as the main agent in changing the behaviour of the child (Clarke, 1975, 1976, 1977; Sandow and Clarke, 1978).

(iv) Summary

Home programmes, group work and therapy can, perhaps, all be seen as aspects of 'support' for the family with a child with disablement. Support generally is often referred to in research. For example, Watson (D: 1972) and many other researchers referred to in earlier chapters comment on the families' need of support after diagnosis. Similarly, Wilkin (1978) argues that parents who have put their children into institutional care did not usually wish to take this step but were forced into it through lack of support. Cull (CF: 1974) writes of the continued need of support for the mothers in her sample and Burton (CF: 1975) suggests that the support received around the time of diagnosis is crucial in determining parental adaptation. In fact, Spain (1973) summarizes the views of many writers and researchers when she writes: 'Inevitably, all families with a handicapped child are subject to increased strain and many families studied were in particular need of material and emotional support'.

The notion of support is clearly an important one and we return to the subject in the final summarizing chapter of this review by considering the kind of support that professionals might most appropriately provide.

CHAPTER EIGHT
Information about Disablement and Services

Information needs

Parents of children with a disease or disorder need information about both the likely consequences in terms of disablement and managing of the child and about available services providing help in management. Other information needs may also be present in specific cases; there is sometimes a need for genetic counselling before conception or birth and for specific information about the initial diagnosis of defect or disease.

However, needs can be defined in many ways and certainly either subjectively or objectively. Subjectively, they can be regarded as 'felt wants'; objectively, reference must obviously be made to some external standard. Information needs cannot be defined exclusively in terms of either category, if only because some parents may well feel a need for information which would not help them much with their problems, while the desire for information on the part of other parents may exceed all possible supply. In general, it is probably most helpful to assume that parents base their care of the child on their understanding of the child's condition and that this understanding is heavily influenced by, and in turn influences, their felt needs for particular kinds of information.

It is at this point that a major form of communication breakdown between professionals and parents often arises. Professionals often fail to meet parental needs for information perhaps because they fail to understand what the parents of a child with disablement want to know. Yet, at the same time, there is a need for professionals to provide information which is important for parents to have whether they recognize the need for it or not. Indeed it may be that the central problems for all professionals in their relationships with clients in which information is imparted, are those of bringing clients to a position in which they recognize that they do need certain sorts of information, and of getting the information across in such a way that clients can take it in. Although there are cases in which professionals simply do not have the information that parents want, there seem to be many more in which it would be fair to say that information is inadequately conveyed. Further, while it makes no sense to claim that professionals themselves should impart information which they cannot possibly have, it does make sense to suggest that they should be honest about where they lack information. It also makes sense to suggest that they have a responsibility to try to ensure that they convey information in such a way as to ensure that parents have a reasonable chance of taking it in.

So while there is evidence that information needs are not always met and that parents are dissatisfied in consequence (Fox, 1975), the matter of parental satisfaction with the information imparted and professional effectiveness in imparting it cannot be settled just by the results of a simple count of satisfied or dissatisfied parents. Even at the practical level, it is not always easy even for a professional to acquire adequate information and supplying it can strain the resources of the best of service agencies (Hewett, 1976).

Information about nature of disablement

The major source of information about the general consequences of the disease or disorder are hospital personnel, usually the consultant (Richards and McIntosh, 1973). Sometimes another member of the hospital team may be the main provider of information. Harrison (1977) found that for parents of children hospitalized with Perthes' Disease the ward sister was the major source, being more available and approachable.

Other workers observe that other sources of information can be important. In her study of children with cystic fibrosis, Burton (1975) found that mothers received most information from the pædiatrician while fathers received most from special literature. In another study of children with cystic fibrosis Cull (1974) observed that the GP was a major source of information when relationships with the parents were good. Sources of information were also investigated by Woodburn (SB: 1973) who found that mothers of younger children relied on the GP and the health visitor, while mothers of older children relied mainly on hospital staff.

In most studies, some dissatisfaction with the quality of information received was noted. However, Jackson *et al.*'s (1973) study of 35 mothers in a clinic setting in which there was unlimited time for discussion suggested that doctors are unable to supply all the information, especially about prognosis, that parents want. On balance, researchers are fairly well agreed that a substantial proportion of their samples could have been better informed and their research, while it is piecemeal, challenges any assumption that the information received by parents is always adequate and appropriate. Thus Anderson and Spain (SB: 1977) observed that 30 per cent of parents in their sample had insufficient explanation of their child's condition; Dorner (SB: 1973) found that only one-third of a small sample (37) of parents were satisfied with the information they received, and Walker *et al.* (SB: 1971) found that, though 60 per cent of parents felt that they had been told enough, only about a third claimed to understand the information given. Hunt (SB: 1973) noted that mothers were inclined to complain of either a lack of information or an overdose of it, with inadequate time being given for adjustment. Finally, Woodburn (SB: 1973) found that only 30 per cent of mothers in her sample had a reasonable understanding; the rest could have been helped by further information.

Data on the information needs of parents of children with other disabling conditions are not so plentiful. Hewett (CP: 1970) found that only half the mothers in her sample had had the condition explained to them. In a small study of 30 parents of diabetic children (Watson, 1970) there were four families who had no understanding of the reasons for carrying out the various procedures necessary to control the condition. In addition, in the same study, eight parents saw urine testing merely as a ritual.

Information on what children experiencing disablement know about their condition is also sparse. In an American study, Collier and Etzwiler (1971) found that the level of knowledge of diabetes among the children studied was roughly the same as that of their parents. Scott *et al.* (SB: 1975) reach a similar conclusion in a small study of the knowledge of 20 adolescents of their disorder and the effect of penile and other urinary appliances.

Teachers with disabled children in their classes may also feel that they need information about the children's disablement. It seems this need is frequently unmet (Anderson, 1975; Halliwell and Spain, 1977; Cope and Anderson, 1977; Watson, D: 1972). In fact, the major source of information for teachers is usually the parents themselves; contact with medical personnel is rare.

It is clear that imparting information is a very skilled task and is much more than a matter of providing relevant factual knowledge. Books, while they can be a major source of information (McAndrew, 1976), cannot answer questions specific to the individual child. Also, as Burton (CF: 1975) points out, written information can be a source of anxiety and distress when prognosis is poor.

Not only does information need to be individual and specific, it also needs to be clear, concise, non-technical and given consistently over an extended period of time (Bobath and Finnie, 1970; Hunt, 1973; Woodburn, 1973). Voysey's (1975) explanation of parental dissatisfaction is therefore convincing. She suggests that the imparting of information is best seen as part of a process by which a coherent identity for the child is produced. Because of the overriding influence of disablement, this process is difficult and unpredictable as compared with that which takes place for the child without disablement. It is not, therefore, surprising that parents want more information than doctors and other professionals are able to supply (Jackson *et al.*, 1973).

Information about services

In the past, several researchers have commented on the lack of information about services provided for parents (Rutter *et al.*, 1970a, b; Hunt, 1973; Spain, 1973). As in many other areas of disablement much evidence is now available from the Family Fund Research Team (Bradshaw, 1977) and by the Department of Child Health at the University of Bristol (Butler *et al.*, 1978). Both these sources of data relate to the Family Fund and the evidence suggests that a wide range of services are influential in providing information. The most important are the Social Services, schools, friends and relations, voluntary organizations and the media, roughly in that order.

Bradshaw (*op.cit.*) also describes an attempt to discover the proportion of those parents eligible for support from the Fund who had not applied because of lack of information. He concluded that about 40 per cent of parents fell into this category and that supplying information increased the take-up rate from 36 to about 50 per cent. Butler *et al.* (1978) have surveyed information requirements relating to local authority services. It seems that 56 per cent of their sample of parents had no idea who to approach about home adaptations – only 34 per cent correctly specified local authority housing or social service departments (those with the most accurate information were more likely to have children with the more severe disabilities). Glendinning and Bradshaw (1977) have confirmed Butler *et al.*'s findings about adaptations generally – half their sample did not know that the social services department could contribute to the cost.

Other findings relating to services reported in the literature include Keeble's (1978) observations that special schools were the main source of information about the provision of aids and adaptations and Butler *et al.*'s finding (*op.cit.*) that only about half of their sample had heard of the orange badge parking scheme. Finally, there is evidence that in the early 1970s authorities were not keen to publicize services in case they created a greater demand than they were able to meet (Social Policy Research, 1973).

Information about government benefits

Commentators seem reasonably certain that the basic knowledge among possible claimants of the *attendance allowance* is good. Thus even in the relatively early days of the allowance Baldwin (1975) cogently argued that knowledge of its existence and availability was fairly good, but that there was considerable confusion about its purpose and aims and the workings of the appeals procedure. Later, Bradshaw (1977) reckoned that at least ten per cent of families with a seriously impaired child who were eligible for the allowance had not applied for it. More recently, Butler *et al.* (1978) have concluded that information about the allowance has successfully reached the people concerned. They report that 92 per cent of their sample knew about the allowance and that their knowledge had come from a variety of sources, the nature of which are shown in Table 4. Butler *et al.* (*op.cit.*) suggest that knowledge of the *mobility allowance* among parents of children with disablement may be less

Table 4: Sources of information regarding attendance allowance (Butler *et al.*, 1978)

Source	%
Mass media, posters, circulars etc.	20
Friends, neighbours, relatives	17
Voluntary organizations	13
Social workers	12
Schools or PTAs	11
Parents of other children with impairments	9
GP or health visitors	9
Hospital, clinic, DHSS	6
Could not remember	3
Total	100

good. Apparently, despite wide publicity, 57 per cent of mothers had not heard of the benefit though these tended to be mothers of children who would not in any case be eligible. Of those who had heard of the benefit, 55 per cent did not know how much it was worth. However, the survey was conducted before young children became eligible for the benefit and payments had been made. Butler *et al.* conclude on balance that there is adequate dissemination of information about this benefit also. They show that 31 per cent of parents were definitely intending to apply and that a further ten per cent were possibly intending to do so.

In general, it seems that knowledge of government benefits may be approaching adequacy, but that relating to other services is not. Thus Butler *et al.* (*ibid.*) found that hardly any parents in their sample had heard of the Disabled Living Foundation. Hard data about parents' knowledge of local authority provision are lacking, but there is evidence that, in the past, the authorities have themselves lacked this knowledge about their own activities. The National Society for Mentally Handicapped Children (1972) employed a research team to talk to members of local authority social service committees. Generally they found a dearth of accurate knowledge about mental impairment and the provision of services. Perhaps knowledge of services for the physically impaired is better. Parfitt and Jobling (1977) set up a resource centre on disablement to provide information to professional organizations about the services available for children with disablement. The centre failed from lack of interest on the part of those working with the children. One possible inference is that knowledge may not reach the parent simply because it has failed to reach the professional. Rather contentiously, it could even be suggested that this failure can be attributed to the professionals themselves.

Information about child management

That parents need to know more than they are generally told about such matters as how to cope with their children's disabilities and what to expect and demand of them has been a common conclusion of research. Thus Rutter *et al.* (1970a) found that about a quarter of their sample of 186 families of children with neurological disorders still had problems of management after receiving medical advice. It seems that the advice that parents receive is of a rudimentary kind: 'take the child home and treat him or her as a normal child'. Richards and McIntosh (1973) found parents anxious because of lack of information on handling. Other researchers (Watson, 1972; Evans, 1977; Goddard and Rubissow, 1977; Harrison, 1977) confirm this lack of information. Egan (1976) stresses the importance of good information while, on its content, Parfitt (1975) has recommended that siblings of children with disablement should also be given advice on how to help them in practical ways.

A major role in information provision is now being played by the workshops and centres being established for children with disablement. Advice is also a central part of Newson's (1976) assessment procedure and is incorporated into many of the units described by Pugh and Russell (1977). Parents' groups have also been formed in which parents inform one another about helpful techniques (Attwood, 1977).

What research evidence on management is available suggests that the advice given is probably adequate, but research on the way in which parents act on advice is also necessary before a firm judgment can be made. Cull's evidence (CF: 1974) is that even when specific information is given, mothers 'experiment' with the treatment regime to some extent so that advice given is not necessarily identical to advice taken. Parents may well interpret medical information in the light of cultural and social stereotypes for constructing meaning and guides to action. Some evidence on this matter may be inferred from the next section in which parents' reactions to information about diagnosis of disorder or impairment is given.

Information given at diagnosis

Aspects of this matter are considered elsewhere (pp. 38–41), but several researchers report that a minority of parents are critical of the way in which information is imparted following diagnosis. Thus Anderson and Spain (1977) report that 25 per cent of parents found the way in which they were informed was needlessly distressing; the proportion in D'Arcy's (1968) sample was about one-third. Carr (DS: 1970) reports that as many as 40 per cent of a sample of parents were dissatisfied with the way in which they were told.

Criticism often arises about delay in diagnosis, but this is often attributable to the impairments being of a kind which is not obvious at birth (Watson, D: 1972). Burton (CF: 1975) records that parents with no previous family history of the condition with a child with no initial symptoms spent an average of a year and a half in obtaining a diagnosis. In Cull's study (CF: 1974) diagnosis took place at any time between birth and 14 years of age with a mean of two years. Cull estimates that 40 per cent experienced considerable difficulty in obtaining a diagnosis and 24 per cent experienced some difficulty. It seems that young mothers experienced most difficulty. Only 43 per cent of mothers and 37 per cent of fathers experienced complete satisfaction about obtaining diagnosis. Cull's control group consisting of parents of cœliac children experienced a similar degree of difficulty, especially when the child was first-born or the parents were of low social class. The major difference between the experimental group and the control appears to have been that the mothers of children with cœliac disease were much more likely to be given the diagnosis on their own (81 per cent against 44 per cent CF) than with their husbands (four per cent against 36 per cent). This seems unfortunate in the light of Cull's evidence that fathers who were not present at the imparting of the initial diagnosis were subsequently unlikely to achieve a good understanding of the nature of the disease.

Some studies have reported an even higher proportion of problems with diagnosis. In Richards and McIntosh's study (1973) of 86 survivors of 289 spina bifida births, it was estimated that only 13 per cent of parents felt that they understood the news at the time of diagnosis and that 50 per cent wanted more information at the time. Freeston (SB: 1971) found that only a quarter of the fathers and very few mothers understood the explanations they were given after the birth.

Several studies record parental suspicion of disablement either existing before information was given or aroused by the manner in which it was given. Hewett (1970) reports that 90 per cent of mothers felt there was something wrong before information about diagnosis was given and Walker *et al.* (1971) report recollections of *sotto voce* consultations occurring between the midwife and the sister in charge of the birth. Woodburn (1973) observes that some mothers were made more anxious by attempts to side-step the issue. Even more serious is Walker *et al.*'s suggestion that mothers may sometimes be asked to sign forms for operation while still in a state of shock.

There is a general feeling that parents should be told of disorder or impairment as soon as it is known (Sheridan, 1965; McMichael, 1971; National Association for Mental Health, 1971; Spain and Wigley, 1975). Thus McMichael records that in her sample 94 per cent of mothers felt that the doctor should tell parents as soon as he suspects a defect. Less extreme reactions arise from mothers in Woodburn's (1973) study: seventy-eight per cent felt that the mother should be told as soon as the anæsthetic wore off. However, parents may have difficulty in absorbing information given too soon, so a once-and-for-all diagnosis and interview is obviously insufficient if information is to be properly absorbed. Parents need to be able to come back and ask questions (Freeston, 1971; Cull, 1974; Burton, 1975; MacKeith, 1973; Woodburn, 1973; Spain and Wigley, 1975).

In summary, the research indicates that clarity, conciseness and adequacy of information both at the time of and shortly after birth or diagnosis can do much to ease the difficulties experienced by parents when they have to face up to what is bound to be unwelcome information.

Information supplied through genetic counselling

Genetic factors are involved in several disabling conditions: muscular dystrophy, spina bifida, cystic fibrosis, and so on. There is general agreement among researchers as to the need for genetic counselling for both the children disabled by these disorders and for their parents (McMichael, 1971; Dorner, 1973; Evans *et al.*, 1974).

The findings relating to the adequacy of counselling for parents of children with spina bifida vary considerably. Freeston (1971) claims that the counsel given was correctly remembered by nearly all parents, while Walker *et al.* (1971) found that only about half their sample correctly understood the implications of further pregnancies. Similarly, a third of Spain's (1973) sample could either not remember the advice given or had not received any advice. It seems fairly certain that about a quarter of Woodburn's (1973) sample had received no advice, while the advice given to the remainder (from a wide variety of sources) seemed to be either inaccurate or inaccurately recalled. Further, Richards and McIntosh (1973) found that, out of 86 families in their sample, only three had received counselling.

The influence of what advice is received is hard to estimate. Timson (1970) has suggested that the birth of children with spina bifida is falling in some areas mainly owing to an increased awareness of the genetic basis of the disorder and increased knowledge of contraception. However, Spain (1973) found that out of 40 pregnancies occurring after the birth of a child with spina bifida only four were planned with a full appreciation of the genetic risk involved.

In Burton's (1975) study of children with cystic fibrosis in Northern Ireland it was reckoned that only 20 per cent of parents had a good understanding of the genetic component of the disorder while a similar percentage had effectively no understanding at all. In Cull's (1974) study carried out in Scotland it was estimated that about half the sample had inadequate information on genetic aspects.

In work on muscular dystrophy, Emery *et al.* (1972, 1973; Emery, 1977) demonstrated that genetic counselling could be effectively undertaken during two or three visits with only a small proportion of parents misunderstanding the risk afterwards. His latest report suggests that parents are becoming more likely to refer themselves for counselling and that there has been an increase in those coming forward from the lower socioeconomic groups. Emery found that parents do not always accept the doctor's word as authoritative; 25 per cent of those in the low-risk group were still deterred from further pregnancies, while five out of the 27 identified as being in the high-risk group for whom ante-natal diagnosis was not available still planned to conceive.

In a study including a range of disorders in which genetic counselling could have been received, Record and Armstrong (1975)
suggest that the death of a child from malformation did not so much
deter parents from further pregnancies as hasten the next one. They
also suggest that the presence in the home of a child with visible
impairments was a slight deterrent to further pregnancies. However,
the tentative nature of Record and Armstrong's conclusions would
suggest that further general studies of genetic counselling *per se*, not
concentrated on those specific disorders, like spina bifida, which
have already been well covered, would provide useful information
about the effectiveness of this provision.

CHAPTER NINE
Voluntary Organizations and Self-help Groups

Introduction

The role of voluntary organizations in providing special services has received close attention from both the Wolfenden (1978) and Warnock (1978) Committees. In the present study the ground covered by these Reports is not reworked. Rather, the evidence relating to parents' knowledge of and involvement in voluntary organizations especially in the form of self-help groups is summarized. In addition, some attempt is made to discuss both the ways in which these organizations have proved helpful to children experiencing disablement and some of the issues which arise from the use of new styles of parental involvement.

Membership of voluntary organizations

Generally speaking, in any sample of parents of children with physical impairment about half will be members of voluntary organizations concerned with the particular disorder or impairment (Hewett, 1970; Freeston, 1971; Walker *et al.*, 1973). Lower figures are usually recorded for parents of children with mental impairment (Moss and Silver, 1972).

Nationally, there is variation round the 50 per cent mark in different samples of parents where children have physical impairment. Evidence from the Bristol studies (Butler *et al.*, 1976, 1978) suggests that some of the variation is related to the particular disease or disorder that affects the child. Thus a significantly higher proportion of parents of children with spina bifida or muscular dystrophy belonged to an association than did, say, parents of children with cerebral palsy. In the 1976 study, Butler *et al.* also report that the parents of children whose disablement is severe were more likely to have joined organizations, but their 1978 study did not confirm this observation. Another finding of Butler *et al.*, in their 1978 study was that out of a sample of 142 mothers who were not members of a voluntary organization, 70 per cent said they were not aware of any such organizations that could help them.

Evidence from the Family Fund studies (Bradshaw *et al.*, 1977) largely supports that of the Bristol studies. In two samples of Family Fund applicants, one interviewed and the other receiving a postal questionnaire, it was found that 57 per cent of the former group and 48 per cent of the latter group belonged to an organization. Again, it was observed that an above-average proportion of parents of children with spina bifida and a below average proportion of parents of children with mental impairment belonged to voluntary groups. The researchers also found that there was some variation in membership between different social and economic groups. Thus membership tended to be higher in the first of the following dichotomous groupings: (i) non-manual: manual, (ii) employed: unemployed, (iii) high income: low income, (iv) two-parent families: one-parent families, (v) small families: large families. Bradshaw *et al.* also report that parents usually join voluntary organizations before the child if five years old, but that there is some tendency for involvement to fall as the child's age increases.

Bradshaw *et al.* (*op.cit.*) also examine the reasons why some parents of children with disablement do not join organizations. About one-third gave lack of time as their main reason, while a similar proportion said they felt that participation was of no use or that they found contact with other parents to be distressing. Another third gave as their main reason either that they were not aware of the existence of voluntary organizations or that they did not know how to contact them. Many families mentioned practical obstacles to joining, such as difficult travel to meetings. Neverthe-less, about 60 per cent who had not joined a voluntary organization were interested in becoming members.

Advantages and disadvantages of membership

Some writers (e.g. Glendinning, 1976) mention disadvantages of membership which may cause parents to be reluctant to join these organizations. Thus Richards and McIntosh (1973) suggest that membership can serve to increase anxiety and frustration; they also suggest that the organizations which parents regarded as most useful were those which arranged practical help and provided equipment. Roskies (1972) found that parents of children suffering the effects of Thalidomide were sometimes reluctant to associate with other parents of these children because of the danger of having to accept the conventional, possibly media-inspired, 'thalidomide identity' for their child. She also observed that parents' need for an association is largely removed if services are adequate. Finally, both Hewett (1970) and Burton (1975) suggest that the literature provided by voluntary organizations, while generally beneficial, can upset some parents.

On the other side, there are many obvious advantages to parents in belonging to a voluntary organization and in Bradshaw *et al.*'s survey (1977) about 70 per cent described belonging to them as very worthwhile. Activities such as providing information, advising about where to get help, enabling parents to share problems and experiences, making authorities aware of problems and providing facilities for children are all mentioned in the literature (Woodburn, 1973; Anderson and Spain, 1977). Glendinning's (1976) transcript of interviews with 17 parents of Family Fund applicants vividly portray these helpful activities of voluntary groups as well as their occasional shortcomings.

Self-help groups

A new element in the work undertaken by voluntary groups is self-help activity through which services are claimed. It seems that, nowadays, parents are less timid about participating in this kind of activity. Stone and Taylor (1977, p. 7) remark that, in the past, parents were conditioned into accepting whatever was offered to them but that the present generation is not so meek, self-help being one of its distinguishing characteristics. More analytically, Nightingale (1973) regards self-help as a change in 'style' consequent on socioeconomic changes in the population at large and experience of the National Health Service:

Suppose spina bifida or cystic fibrosis had been treatable even thirty years ago, and public interest aroused in the survivors. A charity might have been started, but at the instigation and under the control of the public-spirited and monied: the professionally charitable, so to speak, or at any rate the upper crust elite with little, if any, personal knowledge of the disease itself. That would not do nowadays. It would not satisfy the parents of the disabled children, who were themselves brought up under the NHS and are inclined to regard good health as an absolute right. They expect the state to do all it can for their children and they are prepared to campaign aggressively to ensure that it does so. Nor do they see why they should stop there. They urgently want special services, specialised education, research. They are personally motivated and unashamed of the fact: they will not wait for the traditionally charitable to interest themselves in a cause to which they can never, after all, be wholly committed (*op.cit.*, p. 314).

Robinson and Henry (1977) report research by Killilea identifying seven characteristics of self-help groups:

  i.   common experience of members
 ii.   provision of mutual help and support
iii.   the principle that the helper benefits from the exchange
 iv.   reinforcement of normal rather than deviant identities
  v.   collective aims and beliefs
 vi.   emphasis on information
vii.   constructive action towards shared goals

Robinson and Henry would also add that the group should be self-run, should possess a therapeutic ideology and should act as a counterbalance to official groups of health professionals. However, these ideals have seldom been realized in their entirety, though Kith and Kids (Bottomley, 1975; Collins and Collins, 1976; Jones, 1976) is a good example of a group which comes near to doing so. Sometimes associations become professionalized; this can produce strains and restrict development (Robinson and Henry, *op.cit.*). At other times, they may fail to review their goals and expand their spheres of interest (Nightingale, 1973).

Voluntary groups are often perceived by their members as an alternative to or substitute for some forms of official provision, instead of as stimuli to more effective provision. This perception may encourage professionalization. In fact, the research findings on the role of voluntary organizations would suggest that, at the local level, they are much appreciated precisely for the alternative information and support they give to parents of children experiencing disablement. At the same time, self-help groups, where they exist, seem particularly able to extend the horizons of these parents so that they will have the initiative in demanding dynamic and responsible services. However, until there are more of these groups run by parents who have a sophisticated insight into both the perils of professionalization and the need to articulate their aims, there is still a vital need for central and local government, national voluntary bodies and researchers to stimulate legitimate parental demands and to innovate in service provision.

Discussion

We have already discussed at some length the problem of how the parents make their experiences meaningful when these are so clearly not 'normal'. In looking at self-help groups it is useful to look at the way such groups might play a role in helping parents with this problem.

We can recognize, along with Killilea (Robinson and Henry *op.cit.*, 1977), that meeting other parents who share the experience of caring for a child with disablement allows parents to recognize that they are not alone in their experience. It also allows, or potentially allows, parents to voice their sense of injustice collectively. Posing the question at issue in the form, 'Why us?', rather than, 'Why me?', may allow parents to move together towards the recognition that there is really no logical reason why their experience of family life should be so radically different from that of other parents. However, this does not mean that voluntary groups of parents are bound to adopt what may be regarded as Utopian goals for social policy. Such groups often make a strong and clear statement of their acceptance of certain responsibilities, and are usually prepared to take an active part in the provision of services for themselves. But of more central importance is that the collective discussion of issues and problems generally transforms the way in which parents approach professional services. Following discussion, parents are less likely to be prepared to continue in a dependent 'patient' role or to tolerate a subordinate role in discussions concerning the needs of their child or of themselves. Rather, they are more likely to insist upon active involvement in discussions with professionals about their child's care and future. This more active, less dependent, role for parents seems entirely appropriate since only a limited number of decisions in this area need to be made solely on the basis of specialist technical knowledge. Most decisions relate to questions of the facilities available and the degree to which a given local or health authority is able or willing to help the parents and their children. Decisions of this kind are really decisions about the degree to which a given community or council sets limits to the actions they are willing to take to establish a full range of services for parents and their children with disablement. The decisions are, therefore, really 'political' in nature. As such they cannot be simply foisted onto the parents of these children via medical and other specialist personnel.

Hence, if it is acknowledged that parents are, in some sense, to be partners with professionals in deciding the provision to be made for their children then they must be involved in the political processes by which norms of social justice are established. It is one of the strengths of many self-help groups that they are beginning to recognize the strength of this argument and are coming to demand a more active involvement in these political processes. However, to maintain this activity in the present period of economic recession and financial stringency requires considerable strength and determination, and most parents with a child with disablement experience more than enough calls on these kinds of quality. It might even be the case that the spirit of self-help will be broken by such pressures, for the time being at least. It is to be hoped that this is not the case, for voluntary self-help groups have done much to open the eyes of many professionals and researchers to the problems of children with disablement and their parents. They have made it clear that many of the decisions about the future of a child with impairments, disabilities or handicaps are decisions of social and political rather than of a specialist nature because they are decisions about the extent to which *society* is prepared to accept and act upon the view that many people's lives are significantly affected by the birth of a child with impairments.

Discussion touching on this matter in the final chapter of this book will suggest that the effect of the birth of such a child can be described as an unusually arbitrary event which has a significant practical effect. If this is so, the decisions made by parents and professionals on behalf of society are decisions committing society to recognize a responsibility to absorb the effects of these events. As is suggested above, these decisions are political and they cannot be wholly reduced to technical decisions to be taken by professional personnel. Insisting on the political nature of decision-making has been the great contribution of self-help groups. It is to be hoped that, even at a time of cutbacks, professionals will resist slipping back into the 'tokenism' which is a feature of so many professional-client relationships.

CHAPTER TEN
Some Conclusions

Parental perceptions of their child's disablement

In this book we have outlined the findings of mainly British research in the decade prior to 1978 on the social, emotional and practical problems faced by children. Because, as was mentioned in Chapter One, we do not feel that the research fits together in a coherent pattern, we also do not feel that it is possible to summarize the results of many studies reviewed, so disparate in content and methodology, except by referring again to the two broad but quite different problems we identified in the first chapter. These problems, it was suggested, relate to the parental experience of having a child with impairments, disabilities and handicaps and to the general approach adopted within research in this area. In Chapter One, more was said about the latter than the former, in this Chapter the reverse will be the case. We begin, therefore, by discussing the very topical problem at the time of writing (August, 1981), of the great difficulties faced by parents whose child has been born with impairments.

A not unusual response of parents to the birth of a child with impairments is one of pain and despair. The event is perceived as a tragedy. This can be recognized as an understandable response to an event over which they have no control, and which is radically discrepant with their expectations of the normal course of events. In addition, parents often seem to be required by society to present an interpretation of the child with impairments which implies that the experience is essentially 'normal'. Yet, from other perspectives, their experience is far from normal. Hence parents of such children need an interpretation of their experience which reconciles it with their hopes and expectations – and, if society does not provide one ready made, they will develop one themselves. In seeking and developing explanations, these parents are searching for a means of integrating their experience with a social order which denies that it contains tragedy. In sociological terms, the explanations are sought as a means of 'normalizing, controlling and legitimating' their experience so that it is congruent and consonant with the social order. Voysey (1975) puts it thus:

> Evident discrepancies between the parents' situation and that of normal parents are symbolically transformed, so that far from constituting a challenge to, they appear to affirm, the validity of that order. Uncertainty about the future encourages hope, concentrating on the present appears 'realistic'. The inability to take for granted the appropriateness of normal child-rearing practices makes one appreciate the process of child development; even finding out that the child is disabled is better than not knowing or finding out later. Marriages are closer than they would otherwise have been and normal children are found to have hitherto unsuspected resources of maturity and unselfishness (*op.cit.*, p. 203).

It seems that parents are drawn towards theodicies. The inevitable is accepted; miracles are hoped for; good and evil are redefined by looking on the bright side; the 'discovery of true values', 'the positive value of suffering' and the 'positive value of difference' are claimed (*ibid.*, pp. 197–202 *passim*).

Professional and other analyses of disablement experience

This analysis of the meaning of caring for a child with disablement implies that, for the parent, meaning is constructed through categories which serve to normalize the event and to reaffirm the validity of the social order: one can say that the categories function as myths. Furthermore, we can recognize that one potent source of these myths is the contact which parents have with professionals. Doctors, nurses, social workers and other professional personnel will often sanction certain interpretations made by the parent, while associating others with emotional distress or disturbance. This raises an important problem: that there can be no one 'true' interpretation of what it means to have a child with disablement which applies cross-culturally to all parents of such a child. Interpretations are necessarily culture-bound, and in our own culture we regard having a child with disablement as both a tragedy and as something to which parents must adapt themselves by achieving as 'normal' an existence as possible. In other words, through symbolic systems, cultures develop ways of interpreting these events in such a way that their seriousness is minimized while, at the same time, the validity of our assumptions about the natural order of social life and everyday reality are reaffirmed. Hence for every parent there exists a stipulative cultural definition of what it means to have a child with disablement, and his or her definitions and interpretations must approximate to these if they are to be sanctioned.

Recognizing the culture-bound nature of professional responses to these children and their parents produces a dilemma. On the one hand it allows us to perceive that it may be coercive to insist on a rigorous definition of the meaning of having a child with disablement. For example, under professional pressure parents may neither feel able to express their real feelings about the child nor feel that they can complain about any hardships they experience. On the other hand, though we need to be wary of simply offering yet another stipulative definition, refusing definitions altogether is tantamount to admitting that we cannot help parents to cope with their experience. How can we resolve this dilemma?

We begin by recognizing the phenomenological orientation of the discussion above. In so far as this is controversial and political, it is mainly directed against those professional approaches which expect parents simply to come to terms with their child's condition and which also assume that any problems in doing so are attributable to parental pathology. Against the self-assurance of this kind of approach phenomenologists argue that the meaning of an experience like disablement or having a child with it is defined culturally rather than psychologically. They are implying that one cannot simply legislate for a new definition, even one supplied by the WHO; rather definitions are the product of negotiation within social interaction.

Of course, if we argue in this way we are faced with a new problem – how one might change dominant understandings of a phenomenon and what one might change them to. But we need to recognize that we are unlikely to affect directly the answers that parents expect to their central question: 'Why us?' This is not a question which can be answered satisfactorily by pointing to biological or genetic data and by providing a merely causal explanation. These data provide only an answer to *how* it was that the event came about; they cannot resolve the feeling that parents have that there must be reason for it.

Making distinctions between 'how' and 'why' questions is fraught with philosophical difficulties. Nevertheless, we must recognize that people understand events in their lives in terms of both sets of categories. *How* a situation comes about requires a 'factual' explanation in which responsibility is not necessarily attributed to persons. Instead, descriptions are offered of the effects of their behaviour. *Why* a situation comes about requires an explanation in terms of the reasons which a person had for bringing it about, i.e. we are concerned with what people *intended* to do. Hence parents often feel that knowing how it came about that their child has impairments is not enough. Our cultural prejudices towards the impaired are such that we attribute to them and their parents a kind of residual responsibility. Even when parents have, in effect, done something they could not help doing we are still inclined to ask whether they could have foreseen that their action was going to have unfortunate consequences, and we tend to hold them responsible for failing to consider the likelihood of these consequences carefully enough. This is, in fact, the basis of stigma – the sense that some-how, against the evidence, the agent is responsible for his or her condition. In the same way, we hold parents responsible for their children's behaviour. This is simply part of the process by which events in the social, as opposed to the natural, world are attributed by us in terms of the actions and intentions of its members. And when natural events impinge upon the world we still look for reasons, rather than causes, as when we refer to acts of God, and so on. Much as we may wish to see ourselves as Humean empiricists, we must recognize that the world of causality is essentially amoral, and we cannot act in the social world without attributing its features to moral and social categories of intention and responsibility. The question 'Why us?' cannot be answered because there is no reason – there is no 'justice' in one set of parents rather than another having a child with disablement, even if there is a causal explanation.

This is not to say that the question 'Why us?' is irrational or inap-propriate. We can recognize that it is natural to feel that there is an injustice involved. After all, the appropriate answer to the ques-tion, 'What have we done to be singled out like this?', just is 'Nothing'. There is no good reason – the genetic malformation or the biological accident is morally arbitrary. Yet, because we hold that a person should not suffer unduly for things which are beyond his or her control, it is appropriate that we should sympathize with someone who feels that an injustice is involved.

This argument, perhaps, helps us to locate the key issue. For many parents, the search for a meaning is a search for a way of coming to terms with the fact that they are deprived of the 'normal' experience of family life in important respects as a consequence of factors beyond their control. The demand from society that they come to terms with their situation forces them into formulating some way of reconciling themselves to it. A common response is to construct theodicies. These provide a 'reason' for parents', experience by explaining the apparent injustice in terms of some 'higher' justice. The truly professional response, however, is not to supply some alternative meaning for the parents' experience of the event but to alter that experience so that they can live as normal a family life as possible. Successful action of this kind mitigates the injustice, and this, in turn, facilitates adaptation and considerably weakens the need to rely on theodicies.

Too often professionals are drawn into questions of emotional response and psychological disturbance. They concentrate on the way in which the parents come to terms with the question 'Why us?' and fail to realize that it is associated with a profound sense of injustice. More importantly, they fail to recognize that this sense of injustice can be considerably eased by provision to enable families to live as normal a family life as possible. We are not arguing that questions of psychology and so on are irrelevant, we are merely suggesting that psychological answers ignore an important area of the meaning to parents of having a child with disablement.

For instance, it may mean, as the research described in Chapter Two makes plain, extra costs, sometimes amounting to financial hardship; it may mean a multitude of practical problems with lifting, feeding, washing and so on; it may mean social isolation and a disruption of family routine; it may mean being watched over and 'treated' by official agents, such as doctors and social workers, many of whom fail even to try to appreciate the parents' perspective; it may mean lacking the information necessary for receiving the services to which they are entitled, and it may mean accepting low standards of services from local authorities such that, in order to receive even a minimal level of support, parents have to become brash and offensive. Finally, it may mean that, in order to maintain 'respectability', parents must deny that caring for a child with disabilities and handicaps means those things.

These 'meanings' are not always the limit to the personal significance of coping with a child with disablement. Theodicies and their associated despair and resentment may bulk larger in the thinking of many parents than do the more concrete aspects of experience mentioned above. But, though we cannot legislate to determine how parents should perceive their situation, we can legislate to redress some of their disadvantages, and reasonably adequate information, financial provision, support and relief services would serve in some measure to change the practical day-to-day experience of caring. Professionals should therefore do what they can to encourage parents to redefine their situation and take a more active stance to service provision. But, in the last resort, we should remember that the primary aim of social policy for these parents must be to ensure as far as is reasonably possible that their day-to-day experiences are not markedly more stressful and problematic than are those of the parents of children who have no disablement.

In changing the experience of parents we are reducing the impact upon their lives of what is correctly seen as a morally arbitrary event. There is no reason why parents of children with disablement per se should suffer disadvantages which the rest of society does not. The residual prejudices against and stigmatization of such children and their families involve a primitive and irrational attribution of responsibility to them – an attribution which only worsens their problems, and which covertly legitimates the unnecessary suffering which many of the disabled and their families endure. It is a terrible irony that parents should also see themselves in this light.

Parents of children with impairments, disabilities and handicaps are first and foremost parents and should be treated as such. Certainly, the peculiarities of their situation (and that of their children) are inevitably culturally defined and their responses are dominated by cultural expectations about it, but it need not be so different from that of parents who are disadvantaged in other ways.

Definition of research into childhood disablement

Turning to the other broad problem, the disparate approaches taken by researchers and research sponsors towards defining the problems of children with disablement and their families, we remarked in the first chapter of the low degree of generalizability characteristic of the work in this area. Even limited generalizability seems to be ruled out at the outset by the present emphasis on condition-based research. The problem with this kind of research is easily illustrated. Many children with spina bifida, say, experience certain disabilities: how many and which depends largely on the number, severity and nature of their impairments. It is not easy to generalize for all these children and almost impossible to generalize for all those other children who experience similar disabilities by reason of different diseases, disorders, injuries and impairments. In fact, at the level of disability, the undue focus on medically defined conditions has left us with a rather disorganized mass of data which can never form the basis for legitimate generalizations, essential for the effective operation of large parts of the health and social services, about the actual disabilities characteristic of major population groups of these children, such as children of pre-school or primary school age. Not even the still continuing longitudinal survey of the National Children's Bureau, which began in 1959, was set up with this kind of aim in mind.

These considerations seem to lead to two conclusions. First, that each research project needs to be assessed by research managers in terms of the appropriateness of the sample chosen for the focus or overall goals of the project; if research on children's disabilities and handicaps is required, then it is of little use starting with a sample of children with a particular disease. Secondly, that the goals of each individual project should be further assessed in terms of their relevance to certain more general goals, perhaps as described in a strategy document. This second conclusion is obviously the more contentious since accepting it may well involve our recognizing that there is not enough time or money available in any economic climate to undertake research for its own sake into every aspect of childhood disablement. Choices will have to be made within a clear description of a broadly-based research policy.

Such a policy will promote research concerned to discover how far and in what ways the experiences of children with disabilities and their families differ from those of children without disabilities and their families. It will also promote research concerned with identifying the point at which impairments and disabilities begin to have a significant impact in terms of handicap. Research will also be necessary to monitor services and benefits by finding out the extent to which these are successful in reaching their target populations. Finally, research will also be necessary to discover methods by which the problems faced by children with disablement and their families can be further reduced.

To conceive research as having these explicit goals is to recognize that it could play a central role in guiding and assessing the practical interventions of service agencies. In addition, it will encourage researchers to view their work as contributing to an overall description of disablement experience. They will also come to recognize that they share common goals with other workers in this field.

Another practical outcome is that more researchers might be encouraged to choose their research methods and instruments with an eye to the comparability of their data with data obtained from other work. There is a particular need, as we imply by our commendation of the ICIDH, for using agreed definitions and classifications of basic concepts and agreed measuring instruments for assessing the intensity and extent of recognized behavioural states. At the present time, the absence of common definitions, classifications and measuring techniques often undermines any possibility of cross-study comparisons. Certainly, for this reason, we have sometimes found it extremely difficult to compare the findings of pieces of research reviewed in this study even when they have similar aims. Obviously, when samples based on different definitions of the parent population are drawn, when different aspects of disablement are studied, and when different measures of these aspects are used, there is no common basis for comparing data, and the comparisons made are only a little better than guesswork. It is a matter of urgency for arrangements to be made which will allow researchers to collaborate in designing and testing a range of validated assessment instruments for use in future research. It was also observed in Chapter One that a fundamental methodological weakness of much of the research on children with disablement reviewed in this study is that it is often based on small samples and that controls are seldom used. Of course, there is a place for small-scale research to highlight particular problems but it is dangerous to generalize from it. Rather it must suggest hypotheses and prepare the way for larger scale research. The projects of Voysey (1975) and Glendinning (1978) illustrate these properties of good small-scale research. By contrast, and with apologies for our invidiousness, we mention Kolin *et al.* (1971) who drew conclusions that really cannot be drawn from small-scale research when they claim a high incidence of marital breakdown among parents of children with meningomyelocele (a form of severe spina bifida) on the basis of data drawn from a clinical group of only 13 children. The important thing is to ensure that methods match goals. Hence Voysey's (1975) sample of 22 children is enough to draw conclusions relating to the research objectives she specified.

On controls, we regard it as obvious that they are a 'good thing', but we would also mention that the cost of using controls in research can be high and they may not always offer returns commensurate with that cost. Hence a cost-benefit criterion may need to be included among the criteria determining the kind of sampling-frame to be used in surveys. Baldwin (1977a) makes this point within a discussion of the costing of an income and expenditure study on families with children with disablement.

Another mainly technical problem occurring within many studies relates to their use of tests designed for the educational, psychological or social assessment of 'normal' children. There is some danger that tests designed for and validated on non-disabled populations will not measure the same thing when applied to disabled populations. Fair and Birch (1971), for example, have shown that children with disabilities perform better on a series of tests when they are allowed to rest between tests. This result was not observed with non-disabled controls. Similarly, when an instrument like Rutter's malaise scale (Rutter *et al.*, 1970a, b) is used with parents of disabled children, the results may have to be evaluated carefully. Questions designed to elicit symptoms of stress, e.g. 'Do you often have backache?' may really register the physical effects of caring for children with certain kinds of impairment or disability. Hence it may be that certain scales in a test of this kind will measure a different thing when used with parents of children with disablement from that which it measures for those with 'normal' children.

A further plea for a shift of resources from condition-based research towards broader-based functional studies arises from the nature of local government services. In general, an assumption is probably made that these are directed to all children with severe impairments and disabilities, regardless of diagnostic category. The main exceptions are those services provided by specialist charitable organizations. Given this broad concern of local government and therefore, presumably, of central government also, it seems inappropriate to continue with 'officially' sponsored condition-based research unless there is some indication of the existence of special requirements which are overlooked by broader-based studies. If research is to be relevant, and there really is no point in irrelevance, then it has to be accepted that government policy largely determines what counts as relevant. Research has therefore to be orientated to the kinds of question which arise from government policy and when, as in this particular case, this policy seems to be in line with international trends in moving away from an exclusively pathology-centred model of disease processes there seems little point in government agencies encouraging condition-based research further.

A final point concerns what might be a significant lacuna in current research. There is a paucity of research in which the opinions and attitudes of children themselves with disabilities are sought. Certainly, there may be ethical problems in undertaking such work but not necessarily many more than in comparable work with non-disabled children. At present a fair amount is heard from parents (and even this is a comparatively recent venture) and a good deal from professionals about what it may mean for a child to have disablement, but we do not hear much from the children themselves. We look forward to more work being undertaken in this area. At the time of writing, the plans of the Fish Project (Kiernan, 1978) represent a modest beginning.

References

AGERHOLM, M. (1975). 'Handicaps and the handicapped: a nomenclature and classification of intrinsic handicaps', *Royal Society of Health*, **3**, (1), 3–8.

ANDERSON, E. M. (1973). *The Disabled Schoolchild*. London: Methuen.

ANDERSON, E. M. (1975). 'The Integration of Handicapped Children in Ordinary Primary Schools'. In: LOVING, J. and BURN, C. (eds). *Integration of Handicapped Children in Society*. London: Routledge and Kegan Paul in association with the Spastics Society.

ANDERSON, E. M. and CLARKE, L. (1978). Current research – personal communication.

ANDERSON, E. M. and SPAIN, B. (1977). *The Child with Spina Bifida*. London: Methuen.

ARNOLD, G. G. (1976). 'Problems of the cerebral palsy child and his family', *Medical Monographs*, **103**, 225–7.

ATTWOOD, T. (1977). 'The Priory Parents' Workshop,' *Child: Care, Health and Development*, **3**, 81–91.

BAGLEY, C. (1975). 'Suicidal behaviour and suicidal ideation in adolescents,' *British J. of Guidance and Counselling*, **3**, (2), 190–208.

BALDWIN, S. (1975). 'Families with Handicapped Children.' In: JONES, K. (ed.). *Year Book of Social Policy in Britain*. London: Routledge and Kegan Paul.

BALDWIN, S. (1975a). A Study of the Mobility Needs of Handicapped Children including a review of Family Fund Policy on Mobility and an Appraisal of the Mobility Allowance. Social Policy Research Unit, University of York.

BALDWIN, S. (1976). Some Practical Consequences of Caring for Handicapped Children at Home. Social Policy Research Unit, University of York.

BALDWIN, S. (1977). *Disabled Children: counting the costs*. London: The Disability Alliance.

BALDWIN, S. (1977a). The Income and Expenditure of Families with Handicapped Children. Research Proposal. DHSS 13. 4/77.

BAYLAY, M. (1973). *Mental Handicap and Community Care*. London: Routledge and Kegan Paul.

BENTOVIM, A. (1972). 'Handicapped pre-school children and their families (i) Attitudes to the child,' *British Medical Journal*, **3**, 579–81. (ii) 'Effects on the child's early development,' *British Medical Journal*, **3**,

634–7, revised for *Collected Essays from British Medical Journal: Emotional Problems of Childhood and Adolescence*. London: British Medical Journal (1973).

BERGER, P. and LUCKMAN, T. (1967). *Social Construction of Reality*. London: Allen Lane.

BERGGREEN, S. M. (1971). 'A study of the mental health of the near relatives of twenty multihandicapped children,' *Acta Pædiatrica Scandinavia*. Supplement 215.

BERGSTOM-WALEN, M. B. (1972). 'The problems of sex and handicap in Sweden: an investigation.' In: LANCASTER-GAYE, D. (ed.) *Personal Relationships, the Handicapped and the Community*. London: Routledge and Kegan Paul.

BIRCH, H. G. (1964). *Brain Damage in Children: The biological and social aspects*. Baltimore: Williams and Wilkins.

BIRENBAUM, A. (1970). 'On Managing a Courtesy Stigma,' *J. of Health and Social Behaviour*, **2**, 196–206.

BLOOM, F. (1976). 'As Aspect of Social Services for the Handicapped Child in the Community,' *Talk*, Spring, **79**, 22–5.

BOBATH, B. and FINNIE, N. R. (1970). 'Problems of Communication between Parents and Staff in the Treatment and Management of Children with Cerebral Palsy,' *Developmental Medicine and Child Neurology*, **12**, 629–35.

BOOTH, T. (1978). 'From normal baby to handicapped child: unravelling the idea of subnormality in families of mentally handicapped children,' *Sociology*, **12**, (2), 203–21.

BOTTOMLEY, J. L. (1975). Kith and Kids: A Group for Families of Handicapped Children. MSc Thesis, University of Sussex.

BOWLEY, A. (1967). 'A follow up study of 64 children with cerebral palsy,' *Development Medicine and Child Neurology*, **9**, 172–82.

BRADFORD SOCIAL WORK RESEARCH UNIT (1978). Problems for Social Work: Preliminary Report. University of Bradford.

BRADSHAW, J. (1975). *The Financial Needs of Disabled Children*, No. 2. London: The Disability Alliance.

BRADSHAW, J. (1977). Examining benefits for families with handicapped children, in Papers presented at *Social Security Research Seminar, April 1976*, DHSS. London: HMSO.

BRADSHAW, J. (1978a). The Family Fund: An Initiative in Social Policy. PhD Thesis, University of York.

BRADSHAW, J. (1978b). *Incontinence: A Burden for Families with Handicapped Children*. London: Disabled Living Foundation.

BRADSHAW, J. (1978c). A study of incontinence services in eleven areas. University of York, Social Policy Research Unit.

BRADSHAW, J., GLENDINNING, C. and HATCH, S. (1977). 'Voluntary organisations for handicapped and their families: the meaning of membership,' *Child: Care, Health and Development*, **3**, 247–60.

BRADSHAW, J. and LAWTON, D. (1978). Tracing the causes of stress in families with handicapped children. University of York, Social Policy Research Unit.

BRADSHAW, J. (1980). *The Family Fund: An Initiative in Social Policy.* London: Routledge and Kegan Paul.

BRANT, S. and HANSEN, T. V. (1972). 'Young Adults with Cerebral Palsy in Denmark: an investigation into some sexual problems.' In: LANCASTER-GAYE, D. (ed.) *Personal Relationships, the Handicapped and the Community.* London: Routledge and Kegan Paul.

BRIMBLECOMBE, F. S. W. (1974). 'Exeter project for handicapped children,' *British Medical Journal*, **3**, 706–9.

BRIMBLECOMBE, F. S. W. (1977). 'The Honeylands Project,' *J. of Maternal and Child Health*, **2**, 361–6.

BRODMAN, K. *et al.* (1949). 'The Cornell Medical Index,' *J. of American Medical Association*, **40**, 530–4.

BRODMAN, K. *et al.* (1952). 'The Cornell Medical Index,' *J. of Clinical Psychology*, **8**, 289–93.

BROWSE, B. (1972). *The Fares Enquiry – I.* National Association for the Welfare of Children in Hospital.

BROWSE, B. (1973). *The Fares Enquiry – II.* National Association for the Welfare of Children in Hospital.

BURTON, L. (1975). *The Family Life of Sick Children.* London: Routledge and Kegan Paul.

BUTLER, N., GILL, R. and POMEROY, D. (1976). Housing problems of handicapped people in Bristol. University of Bristol, Child Health Research Unit.

BUTLER, N., GILL, R., POMEROY, D. and FEWTRELL, J. (1978). Handicapped children – their homes and life styles. University of Bristol, Department of Child Health.

CANNELL, R. T. (1970). Effects of physical disorder on the adjustment of hospitalised children. PhD Thesis. University of Missouri, Columbia.

CANTER, H. and BARNITT, R. (1978). Research on physical handicap and residential provisions. Unpublished report of pre-pilot study. (DHSS personal communication).

CARR, J. (1970). 'Mongolism: telling the parents,' *Developmental Medicine and Child Neurology*, **12**, 213–21.

CASHDAN, A. (1968). 'Mothers bringing up physically handicapped children.' In: LOVING, J. and MASON, A. (eds) *The Subnormal Child* London: Spastics Society. 194–205.

CENTRAL COUNCIL FOR EDUCATION AND TRAINING IN SOCIAL WORK (CCETSW) (1974). Social Work; people with handicaps need better trained workers. CCETSW Paper No. 5, Report of Working Party on Training for Social Work with Handicapped People.

CHIGIER, E. and CHIGIER, M. (1968). 'Attitudes to disability of children in the multi-cultural society of Israel,' *J. of Health and Social Behaviour.*

CLARKE, A. B. D. (1975, 1976, 1977). Experimental programme for intervention at home with parents of pre-school severely subnormal children. University of Hull, Department of Psychology. Reports 1, 2 and 3 to DHSS.

CLARKE, M. M., RIACH, J. and CHEYNE, W. M. (1977). Handicapped children and pre-school education. Report to Warnock Committee on Special Education. University of Strathclyde.

CLIFFORD, E. (1969). 'The impact of symptom: a preliminary comparison of cleft lip-palate and asthmatic children,' *Cleft Palate Journal*, **6**, 221–7.

COLLIER, B. N. and ETZWILER, D. D. (1971). 'Comparative study of diabetics knowledge among juvenile diabetics and their parents,' *Diabetes*, **20**, 51–7.

COLLINS, M. and COLLINS, D. (1976). *Kith and Kids: self help for families of the handicapped*. London: Souvenir Press (Education and Academic).

COPE, C. and ANDERSON, E. M. (1977). Special Units in Ordinary Schools, Studies in Education No. 6. University of London Institute of Education.

CORNER, R. J. and PILIAVAN, J. A. (1972). 'The effect of physical deviance upon face to face interaction: the other side,' *J. of Personality and Social Psychology*, **23**, 33–9.

CRANK, A. and KELLY, P. (1976). 'Seven points for action,' *Health and Social Services Journal*, **86** (Supp.) 12–13.

CULL, A. M. (1974). A study of the psychological concomitants of a chronic illness in childhood. PhD Thesis, University of Edinburgh.

D'ARCY, E. (1968). 'Congenital defects: mothers' reactions to first information,' *British Medical Journal*, **3**, 796–8.

DAVIE, R. (1972). 'The place of the disabled,' *British Hospital Journal and Social Service Review*, 16 September.

DAVIE, R. (1975). Children and families with special needs. Inaugural lecture. University College, Cardiff, 22 January.

DAVIE, R., BUTLER, N. and GOLDSTEIN, H. (1972). *From Birth to Seven*. London: Longman (in association with the National Children's Bureau).

DAVIS, R. E. (1975). 'Family of physically disabled child: family reactions and deductive reasoning,' *New York State J. of Medicine*, **75**, 1039–41.

DIXON, J. K. (1977). 'Coping with prejudice: attitudes of handicapped persons towards the handicapped,' *J. of Chronic Diseases*, **30**, 307–22.

DOMAN, G. (1974). What to do about your brain injured child. New York: Doubleday.

DORNER, S. (1973). 'Psychological and social problems of families of adolescent spina bifida patients: a preliminary report,' *Developmental Medicine and Child Neurology*, **15**, Supp. 29. 24–7.

DORNER, S. (1975). 'The relationship of physical handicap to stress in families with an adolescent with spina bifida,' *Developmental Medicine and Child Neurology*, **17**, 765–76.

DORNER, S. (1977). 'Sexual interest and activity in adolescents with spina bifida,' *J. of Child Psychology and Psychiatry*, **18**, 229–37.

DROTAR, D., BASKIEWICZ, I. N., KUNNEL, J. and KLAUS, M. (1975). 'The adaption of parents to the birth of an infant with congenital malformations: a hypothetical model,' *Pediatrics*, **56**, (5), 710–7.

DUDZINSKI, D. and PETERS, D. L. (1977). 'Home based programs: a growing alternative,' *Child Care Quarterly*, **6**, 61–71.

EGAN, D. (1976). 'The young handicapped child: a true concern,' *Public Health*, **90**, 3, March.

EMERY, A. E. H. (1977). 'Changing patterns in a genetic counselling clinic.' In: LUBS, HERBERT, A and DE LA CRUZ, FELIX (eds) *Genetic Counselling*. New York: Raven.

EMERY, A. E. H., WATT, M. S. and CLACK, E. R. (1972). 'The effects of genetic counselling in Duchenae muscular dystrophy,' *Clinical Genetics*, **3**, 147–50.

EMERY, A. E. H., WATT, M. S. and CLACK, E. R. (1973). 'Social effects of genetic counselling,' *British Medical Journal*, **1**, 724–6.

EVANS, K., HICKMAN, V. and CARTER, C. D. (1974). 'Handicap and social status of adults with spina bifida cystica,' *British J. of Prevent. Social Med.*, **28**, 85–92.

EVANS, R. (1977). Communication, liaison and support for parents of the handicapped child. (Persoal communication – copy of York Seminar Papers.)

FAIR, D. T. and BIRCH, J. W. (1971). 'Effect of rest on test scores of physically handicapped and non-handicapped children,' *Exceptional Children*, **38**, (4), 335–6.

FAMILY FUND (1975). Basic tabulations of the follow-up survey. University of York, Social Policy Research Unit. F.F. 43.

FEINBERG, T., LATTIMER, J. K., JETER, K., LANGFORD, W. and BECK, L. (1977). 'Questions that worry children with exstrophy,' *Pediatrics*, **53**, 242–7.

FISHMAN, C. A. and FISHMAN, D. B. (1975). 'A group training program in behaviour modification for mothers of children with birth defects,' *Child Psychology and Human Development*, **6**, (1), 3–14.

FOGELMAN, K. (1976). *Britain's sixteen-year olds*. London: National Children's Bureau.

FOTHERINGHAM, J. B. and CREAL, D. (1974). 'Handicapped children and handicapped families,' *International Review of Education*, **20**, 355–71.

FOX, A. M. (1971). Handicapped children: the needs of their families and individual attitudes to services provided. Dissertation for Certificate of Developmental Pædiatrics, Wolfson Centre, University of London.

FOX, A. M. (1975). 'Families with handicapped children – a challenge to the caring professions,' *Community Health*, **6**, 217–23.

FOX, A. M. (1977). 'Psychological problems of physically handicapped children,' *British J. of Hospital Medicine*, **17**, 479–90.

FREEMAN, R. (1970). 'Psychiatric problems in adolescents with cerebral palsy,' *Developmental Medicine and Child Neurology*, **12**, 64–70.

FREESTON, B. M. (1971). 'An enquiry into the effect of a spina bifida child upon family life,' *Developmental Medicine and Child Neurology*, **13**, 456–61.

FULTHORPE, D. (1974). 'Spina bifida: some psychological aspects,' *Special Education and Future Trends*, **1**, 17–20.

GARRETT, B. (1978). Fostering mentally handicapped children. Report to Somerset Social Services Department. Personal Communication.

GATH, A. (1973). 'The school age siblings of Mongol children,' *British J. of Psychiatry*, **123**, 161–7.

GATH, A. (1974). 'Sibling reactions to mental handicap: a comparison of the brothers and sisters of mongol children,' *J. of Child Psychology and Psychiatry*, **15**, 187–98.

GATH, A. (1977). 'The impact of an abnormal child upon the parents,' *Brit. J. of Psychiatry*, **130**, 405–10.

GAYTON, W. F. and FRIEDMAN, S. B. (1973). 'Psycho-social aspects of cystic fibrosis: a review of the literature,' *American J. of Diseases in Childhood*, **126**, 856–9.

GIBSON, C. (1974). 'Divorce and social class,' *British J. of Sociology*, **25**, 79–91.

GIBSON, H. B., HANSON, R. and WEST, D. J. (1967). 'A questionnaire measure of neuroticism using a shortened scale derived from the Cornell Medical Index,' *British J. of Social and Clinical Psychology*, **6**, 129–36.

GLENDINNING, C. (1976). Voluntary organisations for handicapped children and their families: the experience of 17 families. University of York, Social Policy Research Unit.

GLENDINNING, C. (1978). Resource worker project: interim working paper. University of York Social Policy Research Unit DHSS 31/6. 78.

GLENDINNING, C. and BRADSHAW, J. (1977). Housing handicapped children and their families. University of York, Social Policy Research Unit.

GODDARD, J. and RUBISSOW, J. (1977). 'Meeting the needs of handicapped children and their families: the evolution of Honeylands, a family support unit, Exeter,' *Child: Care, Health and Development*, **3**, 261–73.

GOFFMAN, E. (1968). *Stigma*. Harmondsworth: Penguin Books.

GOLD, M. (1958). 'Power in the classroom,' *Sociometry*, **2**, 50–60.

GOLDBERG, R. T. (1974). 'Adjustment of children with invisible and visible handicaps: congenital heart disease and facial burns,' *J. of Counselling Psychology*, **21**, 428–32.

GOULD, B. (1968). Working with handicapped families. *Case Conference*, *15*, 176–81.

GOULDNER, A. W. (1971). *The Coming Crisis of Western Sociology*. London: Heinemann.

GREGORY, S. (1976). *The Deaf Child and His Family*. London: George Allen and Unwin.

GROSSMAN, F. K. (1972). *Brothers and Sisters of Retarded Children: an exploratory study*. New York. Syracuse University Press.

HALLIWELL, M. and SPAIN, B. (1977). 'Integrating pupils with spina bifida,' *Special Education and Forward Trends*, **4**, (4), 15–18.

HALMOS, P. (1965). *The Faith of the Counsellor*. London: Constable.

HARE, E. H., PAYNE, H., LAWRENCE, K. M. and RAWNSLEY, K. (1972). 'Effect of severe stress on the Maudsley Personality Inventory Score in normal subjects,' *British J. of Social and Clinical Psychology*, **11**, 353–8.

HARRISON, S. P. (1977). *Families in stress*. London: Royal College of Nursing.

HERSKOWITZ, J. and MARKS, A. N. (1977). 'The spina bifida patient as a person,' *Developmental Medicine and Child Neurology*, **19**, 413–7.

HEUSTON, G., BACALMAN, S. and MILLS, J. (1976). 'Companion-sitting with handicapped children,' *Children Today*, **5**, 6–9 and 36.

HEWETT, S. (1976). 'Research on families with handicapped children – an aid or an impediment to understanding,' *Birth Defects*, **XII**, (4), 35–46.

HEWETT, S. (with NEWSON, J. and NEWSON, E.) (1970). *The Family and the Handicapped Child*. London: George Allen and Unwin.

HILL, A. (1976). *Closed World of Love*. London: Shepheard and Walwyn.

HITCH, D. (1974). 'The parent. (The congenitally handicapped),' *Royal Society of Health Journal*, **94**, 299–303.

HOLT, K. S. (1975). 'The handicapped child,' *Child: Care, Health and Development*, **1**, 185–9.

HUNT, G. M. (1973). 'Implications of the treatment of myelomeningocele for the child and his family,' *Lancet*, **2**, 1308–10.

HUNT, G. M. (1976). 'Implications of the surviving spina bifida child for the family.' In: OPPE, T. E. and WOODFORD, F. P. (eds) *Early Management of Handicapping Disorders*. (Reviews of Research and Practice, 19). Institute for Research into Mental and Multiple Handicap. Amsterdam: Elsevier Science Publishers.

JACKSON, A., BURGH, A. and WINSHIP, K. (1973). 'The needs of handicapped children and their families in an East London Borough,' *Community Medicine*, **129**, 293–7.

JAEHNIG, W. B. (1974). Mentally handicapped children and their families: problems for social policy. PhD Thesis, University of Essex.

JAEHNIG, W. B. (1975). 'The handicapped child in the family. Block 1. Unit 2.' In: BOSWELL, D. M. and WINGROVE, J. M. (eds). Post Experience Course: *The Handicapped Person in the Community*. London: Tavistock with Open University Press.

JARVIS, S. N. (1977). Studies of Children using Wheelchairs. Report to National Fund for Research into Crippling Diseases.

JARVIS, S. N. (1978). The handicaps and ergonomics of children who use wheelchairs. Doctor of Medicine thesis, University of London.

JOBLING, M. (1975). The family with a handicapped child – research abstract. Highlight No. 17. London: National Children's Bureau.

JONES, A. (1976). Two-to-one: a Kith and Kids community project. Inter-Action Inprint.

KATZ, P. A., KATZ, I. and COHEN, S. (1976). 'White children's attitudes towards blacks and the physically handicapped: a developmental study,' *J. of Educational Psychology*, **68**, (1), 20–24.

KEEBLE, U. (1978). Aids and adaptations. Occasional paper in social administration. London School of Economics.

KEW, S. (1973). 'The cost of handicap,' *Health and Social Services Journal*, **83**, 860–1.

KEW, S. (1975). *Handicap and Family Crisis*. London: Pitman.

KIERNAN, C. (1978). The Fish Project. Personal Communication.

KLECK, R. (1968). 'Physical stigma and non-verbal cues emitted in face to interaction,' *Human Relations*, **21**, (1), 19–28.

KLECK, R. (1968). 'Physical stigma and non-verbal cues emitted in face to face interaction,' *Human Relations*, **21**, (1), 19–28. 425–36.

KOGAN, K. L. and TYLER, N. B. (1973). 'Mother-child interaction in young physically handicapped children,' *American J. of Mental Deficiency*, **77**, 492–7.

KOGAN, K. L., TYLER, N. B.and TURNER, P. (1974). 'The process of interpersonal adaptation between mothers and their cerebral palsied children,' *Developmental Medicine and Child Neurology*, **16**, (4), 518–27.

KOGAN, K. L. and TYLER, N. B. (1976). Mother-child transactions in cerebral palsy therapy. Report by Child Development and Mental Retard Center, University of Washington, Seattle, Washington.

KOLIN, I. S., SCHENZER, A. L., NEW, B. and GARFIELD, M. (1971). 'Studies of the school age child with meningomyelocele: social and emotional adaptations,' *J. of Pediatrics*, **78**, 1013–19.

LANDTMAN, B., VALANNE, E. H. and AUKEE, M. (1968). 'Emotional implications of heart disease,' *Annales Paediatriae Fenniae*, **14**, 71–92.

LAURENCE, K. M. (1976). 'Spina bifida research in Wales,' *J. of Royal College of Physicians*, **10**, (4), 333–46.

LAURENCE, K. M. and TEW, B. (1971). 'Natural history of spina bifida cystica IV,' *Archives of Diseases in Childhood*, **46**, 127–38.

LEVITT, S. (1975). 'A study of the gross motor skills of cerebral palsied children in an adventure playground for handicapped children,' *Child: Care, Health and Development*, 29–43.

LEVITT, E. and COHEN, S. (1973). 'Parents as teachers'. Regional Special Education Instructional Materials Center. City University of New York, Hunter College.

LEWIS, J. H. (1972). 'Effects of group procedures with parents of mentally retarded children,' *Mental Retardation*, **10**, 14–15.

LINDE, L. M., RASOF, B. and DUNN, O. J. (1970). 'Longitudinal studies of intellectual and behavioural development in children with congenital heart disease,' *Acta Pædiatrica Scandinavica*, **59**, 169–76.

LINDE, L. M., RASOF, B., DUNN, O. J. and RABB, E. (1966). 'Attitudinal factors in congenital heart disease,' *Pediatrics*, **38**, 92–101.

LLOYD-BOSTOCK, S. (1976). 'Parents' experiences of official help and guidance in caring for a mentally handicapped child,' *Child: Care, Health and Development*, **2**, 325–38.

LOEB, R. C. (1977). 'Group therapy for parents of mentally retarded children,' *J. of Marriage and Family Guidance*, **3**, (2), 77–83.

LORBER, J. (1972). 'Spina bifida cystica. Results of treatment of 270 consecutive cases with criteria for selection in the future,' *Archives of Diseases in Childhood,* **47**, 854–73.

LORBER, J. and SCHLOSS, A. L. (1973). 'The adolescent with myelomeningocele,' *Developmental Medicine and Child Neurology*, **15**, Supp. 29, 113–14.

LYNCH, D. J. and ARNDT, C. (1973). 'Developmental changes in response to frustration among physically handicapped children,' *J. of Personality Assessment*, **37**, 130.

McANARNEY, E. R., PLESS, I. B., SATTERWHITE, B. and FRIEDMAN, S. B. (1974). 'Psychological problems of children with chronic juvenile arthritis,' *Pediatrics*, **53**, (4), 523–8.

McANDREW, I. (1976). 'Children with a handicap and their families,' *Child: Care, Health and Development*, **2**, 213–37.

McCOLLUM, A. T. and GIBSON, L. E. (1970). 'Family adaption to the child with cystic fibrosis,' *J. of Pediatrics*, **77**, 571–8.

MacKEITH, R. (1973). 'The feelings and behaviour of parents of handicapped children,' *Developmental Medicine and Child Neurology*, **15**, 524–7.

McMICHAEL, J. K. (1971). *Handicap: a study of physically handicapped children and their families.* London: Staples Press.

MARTIN, P. (1975). 'Marital breakdown in families of patients with spina bifida cystica,' *Developmental Medicine and Child Neurology,* **17**, 757–64.

MATTSON, A. (1972). 'The chronically ill child: a challenge to family adaption,' *Medical College of Virginia Quarterly,* **8**, 171–5.

MATTSON, A. and AGLE, D. P. (1972). 'Group therapy with parents of hæmophiliacs,' *J. of American Academy of Child Psychiatry,* **11**, 558–71.

MEIJER, A. (1971). 'Psychological problems of myelodysplastic children,' *Scandinavian J. of Rehabilitative Medicine,* **3**, 113–6.

MILLER, D. R. (1970). 'Optimal psychological adjustment,' *J. of Consulting and Clinical Psychology,* **35**, 290–5.

MINDE, K. K., HACKETT, J. D., KILLOU, D. and SILVER, S. (1972). 'How they grow up: 41 physically handicapped children and their families,' *American Journal of Psychiatry,* **128**, 1554–60.

MINUCHIN, S. (1974). *Families and Family Therapy.* London: Tavistock.

MITCHELL, R. G. and DAWSON, B. (1973). 'Educational and social characteristics of children with asthma,' *Archives of Disease in Childhood,* **48**, 467.

MORGAN, M. R. (1972). 'Attitudes towards the sexuality of handicapped boys and girls,' *Forward Trends,* **16**, 62–6.

MORONEY, R. M. (1976). *The Family and the State: considerations for social policy.* London: Longmans.

MOSS, P. and SILVER, O. (1972). Mentally handicapped school children and their families. Clearing House for Local Authority Social Services Research. University of Birmingham.

MYERS, B. A., FRIEDMAN, S. B. and WEINER, I. B. (1970). 'Coping with a chronic disability,' *American J. of Diseases in Children,* **120**, 175–81.

NATIONAL ASSOCIATION FOR MENTAL HEALTH (1972). 'The birth of the abnormal child: telling the parents,' *Lancet,* **2**, 1075–7.

NATIONAL SOCIETY FOR MENTALLY HANDICAPPED CHILDREN (1972). 'Only 1 in 4 councillors understand,' *Parents Voice,* **22**, (3), 8–11.

NEWSON, E. (1976). 'Parents as a resource in diagnosis and assessment.' In: *Early Management of Handicapping Disorders.* Review of Research No. 19. Institute for Research into Mental and Multiple Handicap. Associated Science Publishers. Amsterdam: Elsevier Science Publishers.

NEWSON, J. and NEWSON, E. (1968). *Four Year Olds in an Urban Community.* London: George Allen and Unwin.

NIGHTINGALE, B. (1973). *Charities.* London: Allen Lane.

OLIVER, J. (1976). A study of 'maternal overprotection' focusing on the work of D. M. Levy. MSc dissertation, University of Leeds. Department of Psychiatry.

OSWIN, M. (1967). *Behaviour Problems amongst Children with Cerebral Palsy.* Bristol: John Wright.

OSWIN, M. (1971). *The Empty Hours.* London: Allen Lane.

OSWIN, M. (1977). 'Physically handicapped children in long-stay hospitals,' *Child: Care, Health and Development,* **3**, 349–55.

OSWIN, M. (1978). *Children Living in Long-Stay Hospitals*. London: Spastics International/Heinemann.

OUSTON, J. (1973). *Children in one-parent families: a research abstract.* Highlight No. 8. London: National Children's Bureau.

PARFITT, J. (1975). 'Siblings of handicapped children,' *Special Education and Forward trends*, **2**, 19–21.

PARFITT, J. and JOBLING, M. (1977). Final report on the experimental project. Institute for Research into Mental and Multiple Handicap.

PARKS, R. M. (1977). 'Parental reactions to the birth of a handicapped child,' *Health and Social Work*, **2**, 51–66.

PEARSON COMMISSION (1978). Royal Commission on Civil Liability and Compensation for Personal Injury, Chairman Lord Pearson. Cmnd 7054, London: HMSO.

PILLING, D. (1972). *The Orthopædically Handicapped Child*. Windsor: NFER.

PILLING, D. (1973a). *The Child with Cerebral Palsy*. Windsor: NFER and National Children's Bureau.

PILLING, D. (1973b). *The Child with Spina Bifida*. Windsor: NFER.

PILLING, D. (1973c). *The Child with a Chronic Medical Problem – cardiac disorders, diabetes and hæmophilia*. Windsor: NFER.

PILLING, D. (1975). *The Child with Asthma: Social Emotional and Educational Adjustment – An Annotated Bibliography*. Windsor: NFER.

PLESS, I. B. (1969). 'Why special education for physically handicapped pupils?', *Social and Economic Administration*, **3**, 253–63.

PLESS, I. B. and PINKERTON, P. (1975). *Chronic Childhood Disorder – promoting patterns of adjustment*. London: Henry Kimpton.

PLESS, I. B. and SATHERWHITE, B. (1972). 'Chronic illness in childhood: selection, activities and evaluation of non-professional family counsellors,' *Clinical Pediatrics*, **11**, 403–10.

PODEANU-CZEHOFSKY, I. (1975). 'It is only the child's guilt? Some aspects of family life of cerebral palsied children,' *Rehabilitation Literature*, **36**, 308–11.

POZNANSKI, E. O. (1969). 'Psychiatric difficulties in siblings of handicapped children,' *Clinical Pediatrics*, **8**, 232–4.

POZNANSKI, E. O. (1973). 'Emotional issues in raising handicapped children,' *Rehabilitation Literature*, **34**, 322–6 and 352.

PRINGLE, L. M. K. and FIDDES, D. O. (1970). *The Challenge of Thalidomide*. London: Longmans with National Bureau for Co-operation in Child Care.

PUGH, G. and RUSSELL, P. (1977). *Shared Care: support services for families with handicapped children*. London: National Children's Bureau.

RAWNSLEY, K. (1966). 'Congruence of independent measures of psychiatric morbidity,' *J. of Psychosomatic Research*, **10**, 84–93.

RECORD, R. G. and ARMSTRONG, E. (1975). 'The influence of the birth of a malformed child on the mother's future reproduction,' *British J. of Preventative and Social Medicine*, **29**, 267–73.

RICHARDS, I. D. G. and McINTOSH, H. T. (1973). 'Spina bifida survivors and their parents – a study of problems and services,' *Development Medicine and Child Neurology*, **15**, 292–304.

RICHARDS, M. (1969). 'The role of the social worker in counselling and support,' *Developmental Medicine and Child Neurology*, **11**, 786–91.

RICHARDSON, S. A. (1971). 'Children's values and friendship: a study of physical disability,' *J. of Health and Social Behaviour*, **12**, 253–8.

RICHARDSON, S. A. (1976). 'Attitudes and behaviour towards the physically handicapped,' *Birth Defects: Original Article Series*, **XII**, (4), 15–34.

RICHARDSON, S. A., GOODMAN, N., HASTORF, A. H. and DORNBUSCH, S. M. (1961). 'Cultural uniformity in reaction to disabilities,' *American Sociological Review*, **26**, 241–7.

RICHARDSON, S. A., HASTORF, A. H. and DORNBUSCH, S. M. (1964). 'Effects of physical disability on the child's description of himself,' *Child Development*, **35**, 893–907.

RICHARDSON, S. A. and ROYCE, J. (1968). 'Race and physical handicap in children's preference for other children,' *Child Development*, **39**, 467–80.

RICHARDSON, S. A. and EMERSON, P. (1970). 'Race and physical handicap in children's preference for other children,' *Human Relations*, **23**, 33–6.

RICHMOND, J. B. (1973). 'The family and the handicapped child,' *Clinical Proceedings of the Children's Hospital*, **29**, 156–64.

ROBINSON, D. and HENRY, S. (1977). *Self Help and Health*. London: Martin Robertson.

ROSKIES, E. (1972). *Abnormality and Normality: the mothering of thalidomide children*. Ithaca and London: Cornell University Press.

RUTTER, M. (1972). *Maternal Deprivation Reassessed*. Harmondsworth: Penguin Press.

RUTTER, M., GRAHAM, P. and YULE, W. (1970a). *A Neuropsychiatric Study in Childhood*. Clinics in Developmental Medicine 35/36. London: Spastics International Medical Publishers and Heinemann Medical.

RUTTER, M., TIZARD, J. and WHITMORE, K. (1970b). *Education, Health and Behaviour*. London: Longmans.

RUTTER, M., GRAHAM, P., CHADWICK, O. F. D., and YULE, W. (1970). 'Adolescent Turmoil: fact or fiction,' *J. of Child Psychology and Psychiatry*, **17**, 35–6.

SAFILIOS-ROTHSCHILD, C. (1970). *The Sociology and Psychology of Disability and Rehabilitation*. New York: Random House.

SALK, L., HILGARTNER, M. and GRANICH, B. (1972). 'The psychosocial impact of hæmophilia on the patient and his family,' *Social Science and Medicine*, **6**, 491–505.

SANDOW, S. and CLARKE, A. D. B. (1978). 'Home interaction with parents of severely subnormal, pre-school children,' *Child: Care, Health and Development*, **4**, (1), 29–39.

SCHAFFER, H. R. (1964). 'The too-cohesive family: a form of group pathology,' *International J. of Social Psychiatry*, **X**, (4), 266–75.

SCHAFFER, H. R. (1971). *The Growth of Sociability*. Harmondsworth: Penguin.

SCHOFIELD, M. (1968). *The Sexual Behaviour of Young People*. Harmondsworth: Penguin Press.

SCHURR, K. T., JOINER, L. M. and TOWNE, R. C. (1970). 'Self-concept research on the mentally retarded: a review of empirical studies,' *Mental Retardation*, **8**, (5), 39–43.

SCHUTT, W. H. (1977). 'Handicapped children.' In: MITCHELL, R. G. (ed.) *Child Health in the Community: A Handbook of Social and Community Pædiatrics*. Edinburgh: Churchill Livingstone.

SCOTT, M., ROBERTS, E. G. G. and TEW, B. (1975). 'Psychosexual problems in adolescent spina bifida patients,' *Developmental Medicine and Child Neurology*, **17**, Supp. 35, 158–9.

SEIDEL, U. P., CHADWICK, O. F. D. and RUTTER, M. (1975). 'Psychological disorders in crippled children: a comparative study of children with and without brain damage,' *Developmental Medicine and Child Neurology*, **17**, 563–73.

SHAKESPEARE, R. (1975). *The Psychology of Handicap*. London: Methuen.

SHEARER, M. S. and SHEARER, D. E. (1972). 'The Portage project: a model for early childhood education,' *Exceptional Children*, **39**, (3), 210–17.

SHERIDAN, M. D. (1965). *The Handicapped Child and His Home*. London: National Childrens Home.

SILVER, D. (1976). *Mental Handicap*. East Roding Community Council.

SKIPPER, J. K. and LEONARD, R. C. (1968). 'Children, stress and hospitalization: a field experiment,' *J. of Health and Social Behaviour*, **9**, 275–87.

SMITH, S. M. and HANSON, R. (1974). '134 Battered Children: a medical and psychological study,' *British Medical Journal*, **3**, 666–70.

SOCIAL POLICY RESEARCH (1973). The Implementation of the Chronically Sick and Disabled Persons Act. National Fund for Research into Crippling Diseases.

SOCIAL WORK RESEARCH PROJECT (1978). *Social Service Teams: The Practitioner's View*. London: HMSO.

SPAIN, B. (1973). 'Spina bifida: the need for community support,' *Quarterly Bulletin of the Intelligence Unit of GLC.*, No. 23, June.

SPAIN, B. and WIGLEY, G. (1975). *Right from the Start*. London: National Society for Mentally Handicapped Children.

STACEY, M., DEARDEN, R., PILL, R. and ROBINSON, D. (1970). *Hospitals, Children and their Families*. London: Routledge and Kegan Paul.

STEINHAUER, P. D., MUSHIN, D. N. and RAE-GRANT, Q. (1974). 'Psychological aspects of chronic illness,' *Pediatric Clinics of North America*, **21**, (4), 825–40.

STEVENSON, J., GRAHAM, P. and DORNER, S. (1977). 'Parental reactions to birth of the handicapped child,' Correspondence, *British J. of Psychiatry*, **131**.

STONE, J. and TAYLOR, F. (1977). *A Handbook for Parents with a Handicapped Child*. 3rd Edition. London: Arrow Press.

STOTT, D. H. (1974). *Bristol Social Adjustment Guide, 5th Edition*. London: Hodder and Stoughton.

SWIFT, C. R., SEIDMAN, F. and STEIN, H. (1967). 'Adjustment problems in juvenile diabetes,' *Psychosomatic Medicine*, **XXIX**, 555–71.

TEW, B. (1973). 'Spina bifida and hydrocephalus: facts, fallacies and future,' *Special Education*, **62**, 26–31.

TEW, B. (1974). 'Spina bifida: family and social problems,' *Special Education and Future Trends*, **1**, 17–20.

TEW, B. and LAURENCE, K. M. (1973). 'Mothers, brothers and sisters of patients with spina bifida,' *Developmental Medicine and Child Neurology*, **15**, Supp. 29, 69–76.

TEW, B. and LAURENCE, K. M. (1975). 'Some sources of stress found in mothers of spina bifida children,' *British J. of Preventative and Social Medicine*, **29**, 27–30.

TEW, B. J. and LAURENCE, K. M. (1976). 'The effects of admission to hospital and surgery on children with spina bifida,' *Developmental Medicine and Child Neurology*, **18**, Supp. 37.

TEW, B. J., LAURENCE, K. M., PAYNE, H. and RAWNSLEY, K. (1977). 'Marital stability following the birth of a child with spina bifida,' *British J. of Psychiatry*, **131**, 79–82.

TIMSON, J. (1970). 'Social factors in the incidence of spina bifida and anencephaly,' *J. of Biosocial Science*, **2**, 81–4.

TINKELMAN, D. G., BRICE, J., YOSHIDA, G. N. and SADLER, J. E. Jr. (1976). 'The impact of chronic asthma on the developing child: observations made in a group setting,' *Annals of Allergy*, **37**, 174–9.

TIZARD, J. and GRAD, J. C. (1961). *The Mentally Handicapped and their Families*. Maudsley Monograph. Oxford University Press.

TYLER, N. B. and KOGAN, K. L. (1972). 'The social by-products of therapy with young children,' *Physical Therapy*, **52**, (5), 508–13.

TYLER, N. B. and KOGAN, K. L. (1977). 'Reduction of stress between mothers and their handicapped children,' *American J. of Occupational Therapy*, **31**, (3), 151–5.

VOLPE, R. (1976). 'Orthopædic Disability, restriction and role taking activity,' *J. of Special Education*, **10**, 371–81.

VOYSEY, M. (1975). *A Constant Burden: the reconstitutions of family life*. London: Routledge and Kegan Paul.

WALDRON-SKINNER, S. (1976). *Family Therapy*. London: Routledge and Kegan Paul.

WALKER, J. H., THOMAS, M. and RUSSELL, I. T. (1971). 'Spina bifida and the parents,' *Developmental Medicine and Child Neurology*, **13**, 462–76.

WARNOCK COMMITTEE (1978). *Special Education Needs: Report of the Committee of Enquiry into the Education of Handicapped Children and Young People*. Cmnd 7212. London: HMSO.

WATSON, A. (1972). 'A study of family attitudes to children with diabetes,' *Community Medicine*, **128**, 122–5.

WHO (1980a). *Early Detection of Handicap in Children*. WHO Regional Office for Europe. Copenhagen: World Health Organization.

WHO (1980b). *International Classification of Impairments, Disabilities and Handicaps*. Geneva: World Health Organization.

WILKIN, D. (1978). Family care of the severely mentally handicapped child and the decision to seek long term care. University of Manchester: Dept. of Community Medicine.

WILLIAMS, J. S. (1975). 'Aspects of dependence-independence conflict in children with asthma,' *J. of Child Psychology and Psychiatry*, **16**, 199–218.

WOLFENDEN COMMITTEE (1978). *The Future of Voluntary Organisations*. London: Croom Helm.

WOLFF, S. (1969). *Children under Stress*. London: Allen Lane.

WOOD, P. H. N. (1975). *Classification of Impairments and Handicaps*. Document WHO/ICDO/REV CONF/75.15. Geneva: World Health Organization.

WOOD, P. H. N. (1980). 'The language of disablement: a glossary relating to disease and its consequences,' *Int. Rehab. Med.*, **2**, (2), 86–92.

WOOD, P. H. N. and BADLEY, E. M. (1978). 'An epidemiological appraisal of disablement.' In: BENNETT, A. E. (ed.) *Recent Advances in Community Medicine*. Edinburgh: Churchill Livingstone.

WOODBURN, M. F. (1973). *The Social Implications of Spina Bifida*. Scottish Spina Bifida Association (Eastern Branch), subsequently Windsor: NFER Publishing Company.

YOUNGHUSBAND, E., BIRCHALL, D., DAVIE, R. and KELLMER PRINGLE, M. L. (1970). *Living with Handicap*. London: National Children's Bureau.

Index

Throughout this index the phrase 'children with disabilities' has been abbreviated to 'c.w.d.'

Author Index